Marketing Analytics **Dashboards Design**

Mastering Data Visualization with Figma and Google Looker Studio

A Comprehensive Guide to Prototyping and Designing Engaging and Insightful Visual Analytics

...because many dashboards drown in clutter and confusion, this book aims to help in crafting clear, compelling visuals that transform marketing data into strategic stories.

Issam Arab

Toronto, July 2024

Introduction: Navigating the World of Marketing Analytics

In today's digital business world, having a handle on data is akin to wielding a superpower. And at the epicenter of this power lies marketing analytics user interfaces that allow business users and decision makers to consume this data or simply "analytics dashboards" – the command center for businesses seeking to navigate their strategies with data-driven insights. Whether it's assessing campaign performance or decoding customer behavior, these dashboards serve as the gateway to informed decision-making.

Yet, let's be honest – creating effective dashboards isn't always smooth sailing. It's more like traversing through a labyrinth of data where wrong turns and dead ends are all too common. The sheer volume of data can overwhelm, leaving us grappling to find meaning amidst the chaos. And unfortunately, the dashboards we craft don't always hit the mark. They might end up being confusing, failing to convey the right message, or worse – gathering digital dust in a corner, unused and unloved.

Creating effective dashboards is like sailing through a constantly changing sea of data. Each dashboard project has its own difficulties, like trying to find your way through a maze with surprises at every turn. The sheer amount of data can be challenging, like trying to see through thick fog.

The process involves more than just handling data; it's about ensuring that the message conveyed resonates with stakeholders. Dashboards are crucial tools meant to guide decision-making, yet they often miss the mark. They might overwhelm users with excessive information or fail to communicate the essential insights clearly, resulting in confusion and misinterpretation. Users may find themselves overwhelmed by data overload or unable to grasp the key insights clearly. This challenge in "data consumption" is a significant barrier that demands strategies for effective communication and understanding user needs to overcome.

Yet, the stakes are much higher than mere inconvenience or confusion. A poorly designed dashboard can have far-reaching consequences, potentially leading to stakeholder disengagement and skepticism towards analytics altogether. When business users encounter dashboards that are they don't understand or fail to address their needs, they may lose faith in the value of data-driven insights, relegating analytics to the sidelines.

However, mastering both data analysis and user experience design presents its unique set of challenges. Data analysts will find it more difficult to grasp the intricacies of user interface design, while experience designers will face difficulties in understanding storytelling through complex datasets. They must navigate through learning unfamiliar tools and understanding their limitations, all while investing time to develop technical skills related to data visualization and dashboard creation. Bridging this gap requires a comprehensive guide that offers practical insights, actionable processes, and a clear roadmap for navigating the intersection of data analysis and user experience design.

As we conclude, design and aesthetics play a crucial role in enhancing usability and driving value. Beyond just presenting data, a well-designed dashboard captivates users, guiding them effortlessly through complex information and enabling intuitive interactions. By incorporating principles of visual hierarchy, typography, and color psychology, designers can effectively communicate insights and narratives, ensuring that data is not just comprehensible but also memorable. Moreover, aesthetically pleasing dashboards instill confidence in users, fostering trust in the data and encouraging deeper engagement. Ultimately, by prioritizing design and beauty, organizations can elevate their dashboards from mere tools to indispensable assets, empowering stakeholders to make informed decisions with clarity and conviction.

Thus, crafting effective marketing analytics dashboards involves more than just compiling data as mentioned; it's about creating an engaging experience. In this book, we will go through the crucial role that design and aesthetics play in enhancing usability and adding value to dashboards. Our goal is to transform these dashboards into compelling stories that empower decision-makers. By focusing on design principles for marketing data analytics, we aim to make dashboards not just tools, but trusted companions that guide users through data with clarity and confidence. Through our exploration of dashboard prototyping with Looker Studio and Figma, we provide you with the skills and understanding to craft dashboards that engage, inform, and inspire action.

What to expect from this book?

This book addresses the common misunderstandings and challenges at the intersection of data analysis and visual design. Often, designers and data analysts work with different priorities, leading to dashboards that may look good but fail to deliver in functionality, or vice versa.

By integrating Google Looker Studio dashboard creation process with tools like Figma and Adobe XD, this guide aims to bridge the gap between aesthetics and analytics. It focuses on prototyping and design thinking to create effective, user-friendly dashboards that not only draw the eye but also provide clear, actionable insights, helping both designers and analysts avoid the usual pitfalls of dashboard design.

1. Prototyping and Design Thinking for Dashboards and Visual Analytics

This book provides guidance on how to apply design thinking and prototyping approaches specifically tailored to the development of dashboards and data visualization projects. It emphasizes the importance of these methodologies in creating effective, user-centric visual analytics that serve as both design and data analytics products.

2. Overview of Google Looker Studio's Capabilities

Dive deep into the visual and design capabilities of Google Looker Studio. This book details the various visualization options available within Looker Studio, offering insights into how to maximize the potential of these tools for clearer and more impactful data presentation.

3. Efficient Use of Design Components with Collaborative Tools

Learn how to utilize collaborative design tools like Figma or Adobe XD to enhance the efficiency of your dashboard designs. This book covers strategies for integrating these tools with Looker Studio to streamline the design process and foster a collaborative environment among design and data teams.

4. Detailed Explanation of Looker Studio Components

Get a detailed look at the different components of Google Looker Studio, including chart types and other elements. Understand their ideal uses and how to tailor their styling and visualization specifications to your specific needs. This part will help you choose the right components based on their functionality and design compatibility.

What This Book Does Not Cover?

Technical Design Skills

This book does not provide training on how to use Figma or any other collaborative design tool from a technical skill standpoint. It assumes a basic familiarity with these tools and focuses instead on how they can be applied specifically to dashboard and data visualization projects.

Data Analysis Techniques

While this book dives into the design aspects of data presentation using Google Looker Studio, it does not cover data analysis techniques or the detailed configuration of data within Looker Studio. The focus remains on the visualization and presentation layer rather than the underlying data analysis.

Table of Contents

Introduction: Navigating the World of Marketing Analytics — 2

What to expect from this book? — 5

- 1. Prototyping and Design Thinking for Dashboards and Visual Analytics — 5
- 2. Overview of Google Looker Studio's Capabilities — 5
- 3. Efficient Use of Design Components with Collaborative Tools — 6
- 4. Detailed Explanation of Looker Studio Components — 6

What This Book Does Not Cover? — 7

- Technical Design Skills — 7
- Data Analysis Techniques — 7

Table of Contents — 8

Part 1: Understanding Dashboard Prototyping — 12

Introduction to Prototyping and User Experience Design Processes — 12

- Core Purpose of Prototyping — 13
- Exploration and Innovation — 13
- Testing Theories and Gathering Feedback — 13
- Cost-Effective Refinement — 14
- Iterative Development — 14
- Contrasting Low-fidelity and High-fidelity Designs — 15
- Defining Prototyping in Dashboard Development — 18
- Chapter Recap — 20

Limitations of High-Fidelity Designs: Collaborative Design Tools & Data Visualization Platforms — 21

- Design Limits in Looker Studio — 21
- Impact on User Experience — 24
- Navigating Design Limitations — 24
- Custom-Built Dashboards Using Development Stacks: A Critical Evaluation — 24

Chapter Recap _____ 27

Data Visualization Processes and Storytelling in Marketing Analytics ____ 28

Foundations of Effective Data Visualization _____ 29

Design Thinking in Data Visualization _____ 32

Integrating Storytelling with Design Thinking _____ 32

Chapter Recap _____ 36

Part 2: The Design & Implementation Process _____ 37

Overview of Dashboard Design _____ 40

Importance of User-centric Design _____ 40

Key Considerations for Effective Dashboard Design _____ 43

Wireframing for Dashboard Design _____ 47

Chapter Recap _____ 48

Wireframing & Prototyping with Collaborative Design Platforms (Figma)_ 49

Tools and Techniques for Creating Wireframes _____ 49

Wireframing for Dashboards _____ 51

Introduction to Figma as a prototyping tool _____ 52

Prototyping with Figma or Other Collaborative Design Software: Getting Started 53

Chapter Recap _____ 55

Designing Dashboard Layouts _____ 56

Principles of Layout Design for Dashboards _____ 56

Examples of Ineffective Dashboard Layouts _____ 57

Chapter Recap _____ 59

Expectation Setting: Understanding Looker Studio Design & Styling _____ 60

Capabilities _____ 60

Design and Styling Capabilities _____ 60

Basic Design Tools _____ 60

Styling Options _____ 61

Transparency and Backgrounds _____ 61

Grids and Guides	61
Image Imports	62
Limitations and Workarounds	62
Layer Management	62
Limited Shape Creation	63
Resizing and Precision	63
Styling Restrictions	64
Combining Chart Types	64
Lack of Animations	64
Interactive Elements	65
Chapter Recap	66

Best Practices for Designing and Organizing Pages in Looker Studio — 67

Device Optimization and Canvas Size	67
Looker Studio Header, Pagination, and Main Layout	69

Looker Studio Theme Settings — 83

Customizing Looker Studio's Native Chart Types & Visualizations — 87

Common Styling Settings	88
Table Visualizations	94
Scorecard Visualizations	99
Time Series Visualizations	107
Bar & Column Charts Visualizations	114
Pie Visualizations	119
Geo Charts Maps Visualizations	122
Area Charts	128
Scatter Visualizations	132
Bullet Charts Visualization	136
Gauge Chart Visualizations	137
Treemap Charts	139
Sankey Charts Visualization	142
Waterfall Chart Visualizations	144

    Timeline Chart Visualizations _____ 146

Building Interactive Dashboards _____ **148**
    Filters in Interactive Dashboards _____ 148
    Integrating Hyperlinks within Dashboards_____ 155

Building in Figma & Translating Designs to Looker Studio Dashboards __ 156
    Step-by-Step to Building High Fidelity Dashboards in Figma _____ 156
    Chapter Recap_____ 159

Final Words _____ **160**

Table of Figures _____ *162*

Part 1: Understanding Dashboard Prototyping

Introduction to Prototyping and User Experience Design Processes

> In this chapter, you'll explore the critical role of prototyping in dashboard development, including its purpose, benefits, and the iterative process it entails. You'll also learn the differences between low-fidelity and high-fidelity designs and their applications in creating effective dashboards.

Figure 1. A digital product prototype example

Prototyping is a fundamental practice in the development of digital products, including dashboards, which serve as critical tools in data analysis and decision-making processes. This technique involves creating early, simplified versions of a product, which are known as prototypes. These prototypes are not complete systems but are essential for visualizing how the new product will function in the real world.

Core Purpose of Prototyping

The primary goal of prototyping is to transform theoretical design concepts into tangible experiences early in the product development lifecycle. This approach allows design teams and stakeholders to explore ideas and concepts without the need to develop fully functioning systems initially. Prototypes can range from basic drawings on paper to interactive simulations that resemble the final product, but are typically quicker and cheaper to produce than fully functional systems.

Exploration and Innovation

Prototyping enables teams to experiment with different design approaches and functionalities. By building and manipulating these preliminary models, teams can creatively explore multiple variations of a product, discovering which designs work best and which do not. This freedom to experiment is vital for innovation, allowing designers to push boundaries and explore new possibilities without the constraints of full product development.

Testing Theories and Gathering Feedback

An essential benefit of prototyping is the ability to test how theoretical design choices play out in a practical scenario. It allows product teams to verify assumptions and validate the effectiveness of different design elements. For instance, in dashboard design, prototypes help determine whether a particular layout facilitates easy data interpretation or if interactive elements behave as expected.

Feedback is a critical component of the prototyping phase. Prototypes are often used in usability tests, where actual users interact with the product under controlled conditions. Their reactions and interactions can provide invaluable insights into the usability and functionality of the product, highlighting potential improvements. This feedback can be integrated into subsequent iterations, refining the product continually.

Cost-Effective Refinement

Perhaps one of the most significant advantages of prototyping is its cost-effectiveness and time optimization. By identifying and solving design problems early in the development process, prototyping helps avoid the high costs associated with making changes after the product is fully developed. Early problem detection through prototypes can prevent the need for extensive

Iterative Development

Prototyping is inherently iterative. Each prototype is typically followed by evaluations and feedback, leading to revisions that improve the design. This cycle continues—design, prototype, test, and refine—until a satisfactory version is achieved that meets all functional requirements and user needs. This iterative process ensures that the final product is as close to what is needed as possible, maximizing its potential effectiveness and user satisfaction.

In conclusion, prototyping is indispensable in dashboard development, serving not just as a tool for visualization but as a platform for innovation, testing, and refinement. It bridges the gap between conceptual design and real-world application, ensuring that the final dashboard is not only functional and user-friendly but also robust and aligned with business objectives.

Contrasting Low-fidelity and High-fidelity Designs

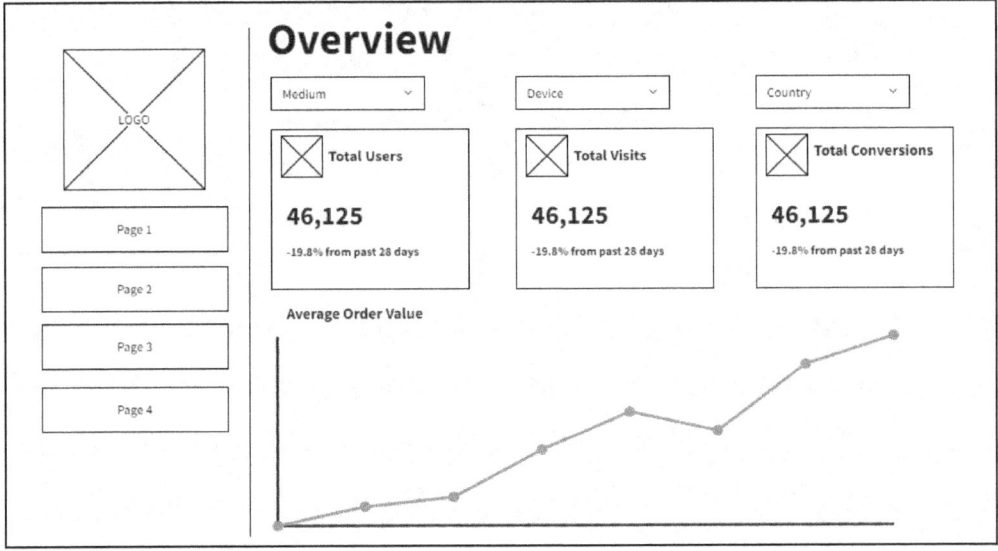

Figure 2. Low-fidelity design

In the prototyping process for dashboard development, designers must use both low-fidelity and high-fidelity designs at different stages, each serving unique purposes in the creation and refinement of the dashboard. Understanding the distinctions between these types of designs is crucial for effectively managing the development process and ensuring the final product meets the intended goals.

Low-fidelity designs, such as sketches and wireframes, are typically the first step in the prototyping process. These designs are quick to produce and are used to establish the basic structure and layout of the dashboard. They are crucial for addressing major usability issues early in the development process. Low-fidelity prototypes are often static and don't include detailed visual design elements, making them ideal for focusing discussions on functionality and user flow without the distractions of graphic design elements.

Low-fidelity designs are the initial steps in visualizing the dashboard. They are typically:

- **Quick to Produce**: These designs are created quickly to facilitate fast iterations. They allow designers and stakeholders to explore different ideas without a significant investment in time or resources.
- **Focused on Structure**: Low-fidelity designs such as sketches and wireframes prioritize layout and functionality over aesthetic details. They help define the placement of elements and the flow of user interactions.
- **Ideal for Initial Feedback**: Because they are simple and easy to modify, these designs are perfect for gathering early feedback from users and stakeholders. This feedback is crucial for refining the dashboard's structure before more detailed design work begins.

Figure 3. High-fidelity design

High-fidelity designs, including detailed mockups and interactive prototypes, are developed once the basic user interface structure is well understood. These designs incorporate visual elements such as color schemes, fonts, and more precise spacing, which mimic the final product's look and feel. High-fidelity prototypes can be interactive, allowing users to click through to see how the actual dashboard will work. They are excellent for evaluating the dashboard's effectiveness in a real-world scenario and are essential for gathering detailed user feedback on the visual and interactive aspects of the product.

They usually are:

- **Detailed and Realistic**: These designs incorporate actual colors, fonts, and other design elements that will be used in the final dashboard. They provide a realistic preview of how the dashboard will look and feel.
- **Interactive Elements**: Unlike low-fidelity prototypes, high-fidelity prototypes often include interactivity, allowing users to click, scroll, and interact as they would with the final product. This interaction is vital for testing usability and the overall user experience.
- **Useful for Final Testing and Validation**: High-fidelity prototypes are essential for conducting detailed user testing and validation. They help ensure that every aspect of the dashboard works as intended and is optimally designed for the

In practice, both low-fidelity and high-fidelity prototyping are crucial. Starting with low-fidelity designs allows for quick exploration of concepts and layouts without significant commitment. As the design matures, transitioning to high-fidelity prototypes helps refine these concepts into a polished, interactive experience that can be thoroughly tested before launch.

Defining Prototyping in Dashboard Development

In product and dashboard development, effective prototyping is the crucial method for visualizing success of the final outcome of how the data interfaces and interactions would function before the final version is built.

Visualizing Data Interfaces

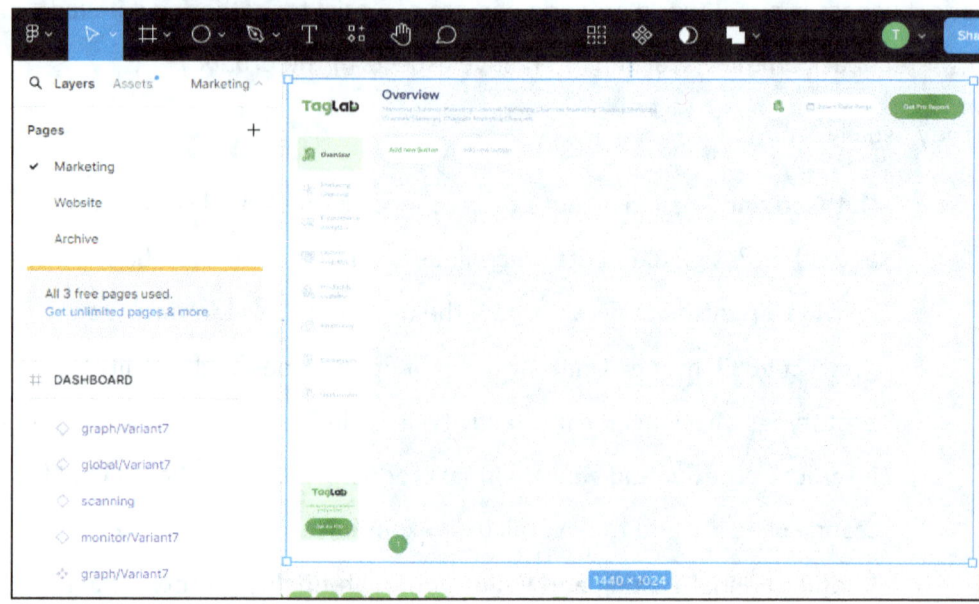

Figure 4. Dashboard main interface designed in Figma

The primary goal of prototyping in dashboard development is to establish a clear and functional design that displays data effectively. By creating prototypes, analysts and designers can test various layouts and interface elements, to see how they can collaborate to display complex data sets. For example, a prototype might explore how a trendline chart average order value over time, or how a pie chart shows user accesses through different device types. These visual prototypes help in deciding which types of data presentation components will be most effective for the dashboard's goals.

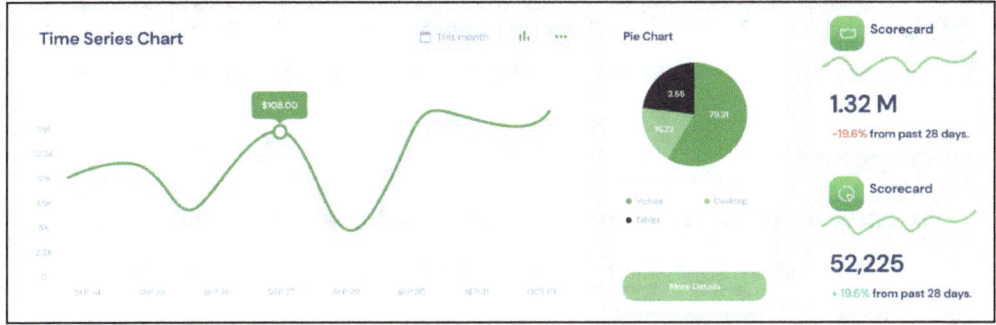

Figure 5. Chart single components designed in Figma

Experimenting with Interactivity

Interactive prototypes can go beyond static images to include elements that users can interact with, such as sliders, buttons, or filters. For instance, designers can prototype a sequence where users filter a dataset based on specific parameters to see how intuitively the process flows and how quickly the dashboard responds.

- **Basic Sketches**: These are often the first step and involve simple drawings that outline the fundamental structure of the dashboard. They are quick to produce and useful for initial discussions about layout and content prioritization.
- **Wireframes & Interactive Models**: More detailed than sketches, wireframes provide a blueprint of the dashboard's architecture without detailed design elements like color or typography. They focus on functionality and layout. More advanced prototypes can simulate final product's look and feel, incorporating user interaction.

User experience design is vital in creating dashboards because it directly influences how effectively a user can interact with the tool. A well-designed dashboard isn't just aesthetically pleasing; it makes the process of finding, understanding, and analyzing data as intuitive as possible. Good UX design ensures that the dashboard is accessible, easy to navigate, and aligns with the user's needs, ultimately aiding in quick decision-making based on data insights.

Chapter Recap

Prototyping breathes life into abstract concepts, swiftly transforming them into experiential prototypes that pave the way for innovative solutions and rapid iterations:

• It serves as a creative playground for designers to explore and refine various designs, ensuring the final product not only meets but exceeds user expectations.

• Effective prototyping is a strategic tool that uncovers potential pitfalls early, optimizing both time and costs by enabling adjustments before full-scale development.

• This iterative process continuously evolves through feedback, progressively enhancing the product until it achieves perfection in functionality and user engagement.

• From the simplicity of low-fidelity sketches to the rich detail of high-fidelity prototypes, each stage of prototyping is crucial in sculpting a dashboard that is not just functional but also intuitively aligns with user needs, ensuring a seamless and engaging user experience.

Limitations of High-Fidelity Designs: Collaborative Design Tools & Data Visualization Platforms

> This chapter goes through the limitations and trade-offs of using different tools for high-fidelity dashboard design, specifically contrasting Looker Studio. High-fidelity designs showcase the limitations of tools like Looker Studio, particularly in areas such as advanced animations, interactivity, and custom element styling, which can restrict creative freedom and affect the user experience, or ultimately produce designs that can't be executed.

The choice of tools can significantly influence both the design process and the end result. High-fidelity designs, which are detailed and interactive models of the final product, bring to light the capabilities and constraints of the design tools used. This chapter explores the limitations and trade-offs involved when using different tools for dashboard design, specifically contrasting Looker Studio, Figma, and custom dashboard solutions.

High-fidelity designs aim to replicate the final product as closely as possible, including its look, feel, and interactivity. This level of detail requires robust design tools that can match the vision of the dashboard with technical feasibility.

Design Limits in Looker Studio

Looker Studio is highly regarded for its robust data integration capabilities with Google products and its array of built-in visualization components. However, it has notable limitations in design customization that can impact the aesthetic and functional quality of dashboards, especially when compared to more versatile design tools like Figma.

While Looker Studio excels in straightforward dashboard functionalities, it often falls short in supporting the advanced design elements that are critical for creating modern, user-friendly interfaces. These limitations include:

Limited Support for Advanced Animations and Interactivity

Looker Studio lacks comprehensive options for implementing sophisticated animations and interactive features that can make a dashboard feel dynamic and engaging. This includes transitions, motion effects, and other visual enhancements that contribute to a smooth and interactive user experience.

Restricted Interactive Elements

Essential interactive elements like hover effects, which provide users with additional information or actions without cluttering the interface, are limited in Looker Studio. Moreover, the platform's support for dynamic interactions, such as elements that adjust based on user inputs or actions, is quite basic. This restricts the ability to create intuitive and responsive interfaces that adapt to user needs.

Constrained Element Creation and Styling Flexibility

Looker Studio provides a basic toolkit for designing elements, which can hinder the creation of custom, sophisticated elements that align with specific branding or design standards. The platform's styling options are also limited, making it challenging to fully customize the appearance of a dashboard to meet precise aesthetic preferences.

Lack of Modern UI Components

Modern user interface components such as collapsible menus, dropdowns, toggle switches, and responsive design elements are not readily implemented in Looker Studio. This limitation can make it difficult to achieve a polished, contemporary look and feel, as well as impact the usability and accessibility of the dashboard.

Absence of Responsive Design Support

In today's multi-device landscape, responsiveness is crucial for any digital interface. Looker Studio's static layout system does not adapt well to different screen sizes or resolutions, potentially leading to a suboptimal viewing experience on mobile devices or smaller screens.

Lack of HTML and CSS Integration

In Looker Studio, the scope for incorporating custom HTML and CSS is inexistent. This limitation significantly hinders the ability to fine-tune the dashboard's visual presentation and layout beyond the predefined styles and formats. Custom HTML and CSS enable precise control over the styling elements, including fonts, colors, spacing, and more, which are crucial for aligning the dashboard's design with corporate branding or specific design guidelines.

No Support for JavaScript

JavaScript plays a critical role in modern web design, particularly in enhancing interactivity and functionality. Looker Studio does not support custom JavaScript, which restricts the ability to implement interactive features such as dynamic content updates, custom user interactions, and animations that respond to user behavior. Without JavaScript, creating a dynamic and engaging user experience is challenging, as the interactivity of the dashboard is limited to the built-in functionalities provided by Looker Studio.

Impact on User Experience

These design constraints can significantly inhibit creative expression and innovation, leading to dashboards that, while functional, do not engage users effectively or deliver an optimal user experience. The lack of modern UI elements and limited interaction capabilities mean that dashboards may not only appear outdated but also operate in a less intuitive manner.

Furthermore, the inability to implement a responsive design means that users accessing the dashboard on mobile devices or other non-standard screens may find the experience lacking, potentially decreasing user engagement and satisfaction.

Navigating Design Limitations

Designers at this point must often employ creative solutions or integrate other tools to circumvent these limitations, which can complicate the development process and affect project timelines. Recognizing and planning for these constraints early in the design phase is crucial for setting realistic expectations and delivering a dashboard that balances functionality with user-centric design.

In summary, while Looker Studio is indispensable for data-driven visualizations and has certain strengths in dashboard creation, its limitations in supporting advanced design elements and modern interactivity can pose challenges for designers aiming to create cutting-edge, fully responsive dashboards.

Custom-Built Dashboards Using Development Stacks: A Critical Evaluation

Custom-built dashboards using dedicated development stacks allow for high levels of customization in both design and functionality. However, this approach often entails significant challenges that may outweigh its benefits, particularly when compared to platforms like Looker Studio, which offer extensive integration capabilities and community support.

Limited Integration Capabilities

Contrary to platforms like Looker Studio that benefit from Google's robust data connectors and active community contributions, custom-built dashboards often struggle with integration issues. Developing connections to various data sources typically requires extensive custom coding and ongoing maintenance, which can be resource-intensive and error-prone. Without the extensive ecosystem of pre-built connectors available in Looker Studio, integrating a custom dashboard with diverse data systems can become a significant bottleneck.

Resource Intensity and High Costs

The development of custom dashboards demands a considerable allocation of resources. Skilled developers, designers, and data specialists are needed to build and maintain custom solutions, leading to high upfront and ongoing costs. This makes custom development a costly venture compared to utilizing an established platform like Looker Studio.

Complexity in Development and Maintenance

Building a dashboard from the ground up introduces complexity not just in initial development but also in its maintenance. Custom solutions must be continuously updated to adapt to new technologies and security threats, adding to the operational overhead.

Challenges in Timely and Accurate Development

Many organizations lack the necessary expertise or underestimate the complexities involved in creating a custom dashboard, leading to projects that often exceed timelines and budgets. The accuracy and functionality of the developed dashboard can suffer, resulting in tools that may not meet the intended specifications or needs of the business.

Scalability and Reliability Concerns

Scalability poses another significant challenge for custom dashboards. As business needs grow and data volumes increase, scaling a custom solution to accommodate this growth can be technically challenging and costly. Moreover, the reliability of a custom-built system, without the extensive testing and community feedback that platforms like Looker Studio benefit from, can be questionable.

Balancing the Trade-offs

While the idea of a tailor-made dashboard may appear attractive due to the potential for perfect customization, the reality involves balancing these significant drawbacks. For most organizations, the high costs, complex development process, and challenges in maintenance and integration make custom-built solutions less feasible. Platforms like Looker Studio not only reduce these burdens by providing robust, ready-to-use integration capabilities, but also ensure that dashboards can be developed, scaled, and maintained more efficiently.

In conclusion, organizations must carefully evaluate their capacity to handle the demands of custom dashboard development against the benefits of using established platforms with strong integration capabilities and community support. In many cases, the latter may provide a more practical, cost-effective, and reliable solution.

Chapter Recap

- While Looker Studio simplifies data integration, its limited dynamic and animation capabilities require creative solutions to captivate users.
- You can push the boundaries of Looker Studio's UI customization limits by exploring the details of its possible features to use them with your own creativity to align your dashboards with your unique brand and design standards.

Data Visualization Processes and Storytelling in Marketing Analytics

> In this chapter, you will discover how to effectively visualize data and craft compelling stories in marketing analytics, transforming complex datasets into clear and actionable insights.

In the ever-evolving landscape of marketing analytics, the ability to effectively visualize data and craft compelling stories around it is not just advantageous—it's essential. Data visualization and storytelling transcend traditional data analysis by not only presenting numbers and trends but by bringing these figures to life, making them understandable and actionable. These techniques enable marketers and analysts to distill complex datasets into clear visual narratives that can inform strategic decisions and inspire action.

Effective data visualization simplifies complexity. It transforms raw, often voluminous data into accessible insights that can be quickly grasped. This is particularly critical in marketing, where decisions need to be made rapidly and are often based on analyzing patterns from large amounts of consumer data. By effectively visualizing this data, marketers can identify trends, track marketing campaign performance, understand consumer behavior, and predict market changes more efficiently.

Storytelling, on the other hand, is what makes these data visualizations resonate with stakeholders. It is the thread that connects data points in a meaningful way, turning abstract numbers into compelling narratives. Well-crafted stories can illuminate relationships and trends within the data that might not be immediately obvious. They provide context and relevance, helping stakeholders understand not just what is happening, but why it matters to them. This narrative approach is crucial because it engages the audience emotionally, making the insights more memorable and persuasive, thus driving stronger and more informed business decisions.

Together, data visualization and storytelling equip businesses with the power to leverage their data more effectively, translating complex information into a clear, visual format backed by narratives that not only inform but also inspire and persuade. This chapter will delve into the foundational principles of effective data visualization and explore advanced storytelling techniques that can enhance how insights are communicated and acted upon in the realm of marketing analytics.

Foundations of Effective Data Visualization

Effective data visualization is both an art and a science. It requires a deep understanding of visual principles as well as an awareness of how information is best processed by the human brain. This section explores the core principles of visualization and how they can be utilized to enhance the clarity and impact of data, particularly within the context of marketing analytics.

Understanding Core Visualization Principles

Clarity and Impact of Visual Elements

The primary goal of data visualization is to clarify the data, making complex information easier to understand and interpret. Key visual elements—color, form, and layout—play crucial roles in achieving this clarity:

- **Color**: Color can draw attention, group related items, indicate relationships, and signify categories. Choosing the right color palette can highlight important data points and guide the viewer's eye to the most important parts of the visualization.

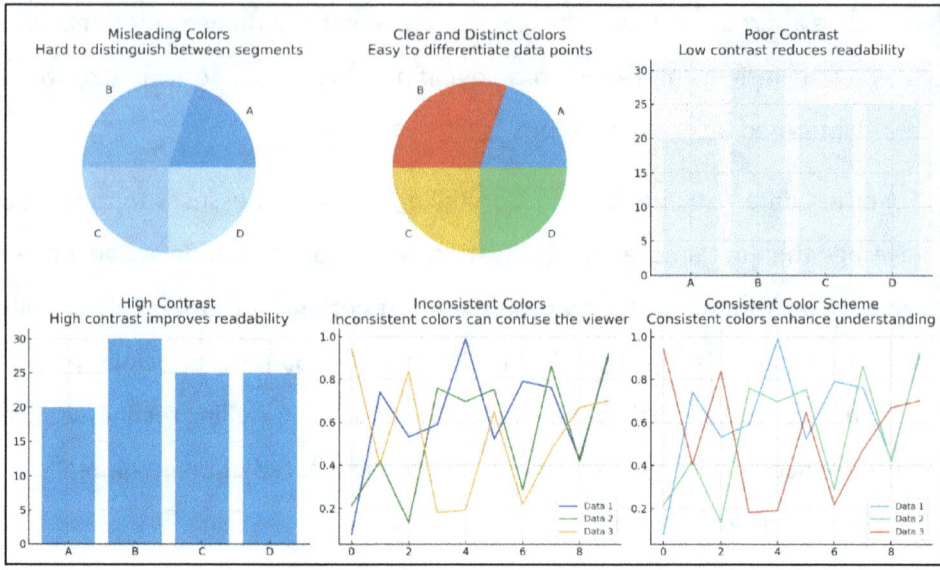

Figure 6. Impact of color in dashboard design

- Form: The shapes and sizes of visual elements in a dashboard should help convey the correct message. For instance, bars might be used for comparisons, while lines could indicate changes over time. The form should always support the function of the data being represented.

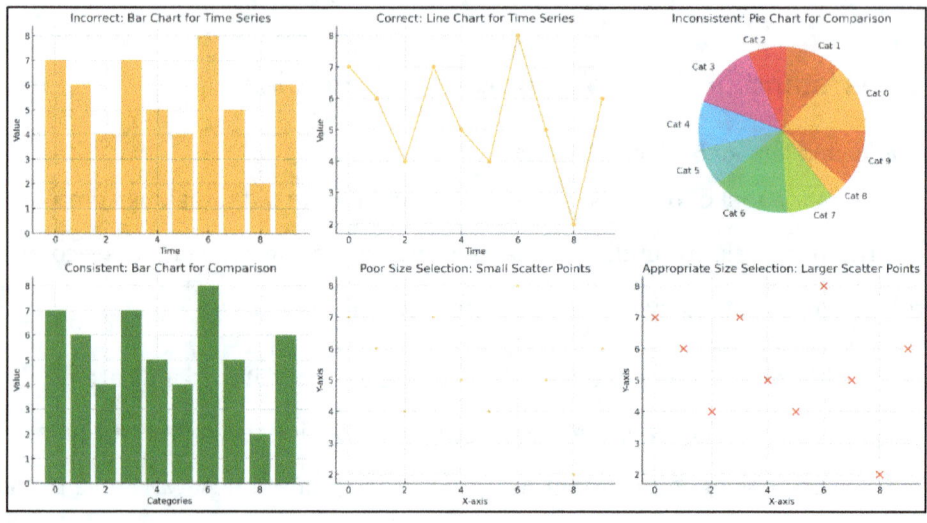

Figure 7. Importance of suitable chart type selection

- **Layout**: A well-planned layout helps in navigating the data visually. It organizes information hierarchically, leading the viewer naturally through the data in a way that makes sense, from the most general to the specific, or from the most important to the least.

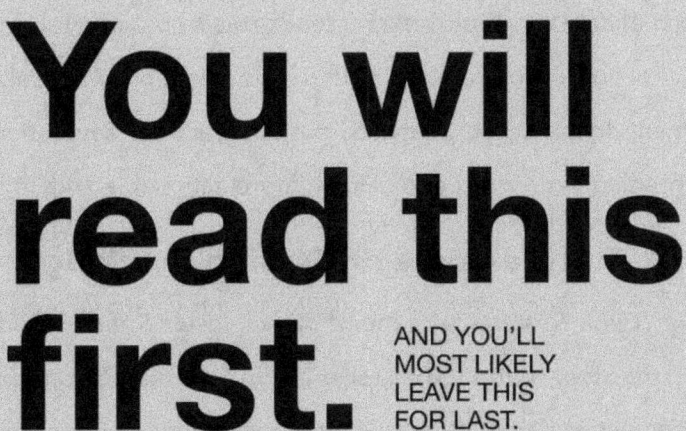

Figure 8. Visual hierarchy impact

Engagement and Understanding

Visualizations must not only present data but also engage viewers and promote understanding. This involves balancing aesthetic elements with functionality to create clean, attractive visualizations that do not sacrifice readability for style. Use relevant icons and visuals for example to make easier for your users to comprehend the data context behind the visualizations or numbers shown.

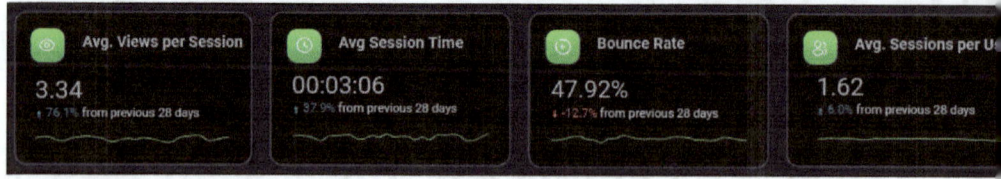

Figure 9. Appropriate use of icons and titles to describe charts' content

Design Thinking in Data Visualization

Design thinking in data visualization transcends traditional analysis, introducing a methodological approach that emphasizes innovation, problem-solving, and user engagement. In marketing analytics, this approach can revolutionize how data is presented and interpreted, making it more actionable and impactful.

Integrating Storytelling with Design Thinking

Applying design thinking starts with the narrative. Instead of merely displaying data, focus on the story that the data tells. This involves understanding the audience's perspective and crafting visualizations that guide them through a data-driven story. Techniques such as storyboarding can be employed to map out the narrative flow before any actual data visualization design begins.

Contextual Relevance

Each visualization should be designed with its usage context in mind. Design thinking encourages a deep dive into the environment where the dashboard will be used. For marketing teams, this could mean creating visualizations that adapt to different campaigns or market segments, making the data not only accessible but also directly relevant to specific marketing scenarios.

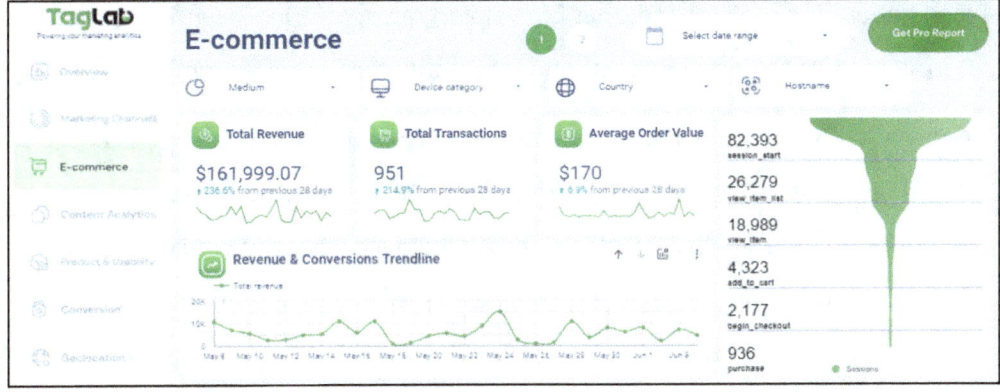

Figure 10. Marketing dashboard with appropriate chart types such as a marketing funnel, and other relevant visualizations with proper titles and icons

Leveraging User Feedback Loops & Iterative Prototyping

In line with design thinking principles, iterative prototyping is crucial. Start with basic mockups of data visualizations and evolve them through multiple iterations based on user feedback. This process helps refine the visualizations to better meet the needs and preferences of end-users, ensuring that the final products are both functional and user-friendly.

Empathy Maps and User Persona

Conduct workshops or meeting sessions to create empathy maps and user personas. These tools are invaluable in visualizing the diverse needs, experiences, and behaviors of the target audience, guiding the design of dashboards to align effectively with user expectations and specific business objectives.

For example, a marketing team might require detailed dashboards that track campaign performance metrics, such as click-through rates, conversion rates, and social media engagement. These insights help them understand the nuances of campaign effectiveness and optimize strategies in real-time. Contrastingly, a sales manager might benefit from a dashboard that focuses on lead generation metrics and sales conversion rates, offering insights that are critical for managing sales teams and forecasting future sales trends.

Another scenario could involve a customer service manager who needs a dashboard that provides real-time data on customer satisfaction scores, response times, and issue resolution rates. Such a dashboard would help them monitor team performance and identify areas for improvement in customer service processes.

In each case, empathy maps and user personas help to tailor the dashboard's design to meet the specific informational needs and decision-making styles of different users within the organization. By considering these varied perspectives, dashboards can be crafted to ensure they provide relevant and actionable insights tailored to each user group, enhancing the overall effectiveness and usability of the analytics tool.

Cross-disciplinary Collaboration

In the context of marketing analytics, involving professionals from various fields can significantly enrich the dashboard design process. For example, integrating insights from media agencies or advertising technology teams can be crucial when designing dashboards focused on campaign Return on Ad Spend (ROAS). Similarly, collaboration with the CRM team can provide valuable insights for a lead generation dashboard. This cross-disciplinary collaboration ensures that the dashboards are not only technically feasible but also contextually rich and aligned with specific business functions. By bringing together UX/UI designers, data scientists, and marketing strategists, along with field-specific experts, the final designs are more likely to address the nuanced needs of different business units effectively.

These refined feedbacks from direct dashboard users or topically related teams emphasize the practical application of design thinking and collaborative approaches in creating data visualizations that are both functional and strategically aligned with business objectives across the entire organization. They highlight the importance of understanding user needs at various organizational or managerial levels and the necessity of leveraging dashboard creation capabilities effectively.

Experimental Layouts and Interactions

Encourage experimentation with different layouts and interactive elements. For instance, integrating interactive filters or sliders can allow users to customize their view of the data, providing a more interactive and engaging experience. However, it's essential to remember the limitations of the platform being used, such as Looker Studio. Users must be familiar with the features available on the platform, like slider metrics or dimension drill-downs. If users are not well-acquainted with Looker Studio's capabilities, incorporating visual aids and tooltips within the dashboard can significantly enhance the user experience by guiding them through the functionalities available.

Chapter Recap

Engaging Stakeholders

- Use storytelling to make data meaningful.
- Make insights memorable and persuasive.

Core Visualization Principles

- Highlight key data with color and form.
- Organize information hierarchically.

Design Thinking

- Focus on the data narrative.
- Design with user context in mind.

Iterative Prototyping

- Refine designs with user feedback.
- Tailor design using empathy maps and personas.

Collaboration

- Integrate insights from various professionals and team members.
- Enrich design through cross-disciplinary collaboration.

Experimental Layouts

- Enhance user experience with interactive elements.
- Guide users with visual aids and tooltips.

Part 2: The Design & Implementation Process

Creating effective dashboards as mentioned previously is both an art and a science. It requires a meticulous blend of visual design principles, user experience considerations, and a deep understanding of data visualization techniques. This section is dedicated to guiding you through the practical steps of designing and implementing dashboards using collaborative design tools such as Figma and Google Looker Studio. The aim is to provide you with a comprehensive framework to create dashboards that are not only visually appealing but also highly functional and user-centric.

Dashboards serve as the interface between data and decision-making, providing a visual summary of key metrics and trends that can influence business strategies. However, the true value of a dashboard lies in its ability to present complex information in a clear, concise, and engaging manner. This is where the design process becomes paramount.

Designing a dashboard begins with understanding its purpose and the audience it serves. Different users have different type of needs; a C-level executive might require a high-level overview with key performance indicators (KPIs), while a marketing manager might need detailed breakdowns of campaign performance. By identifying these needs early in the design process, you can tailor your dashboard to provide relevant insights to each user group. This user-centric approach is the foundation of effective dashboard design.

The first step in the design process is wireframing. Wireframes act as the blueprint for your dashboard, outlining the structure and layout without getting into the visual details. This allows you to focus on the functional aspects, ensuring that the information is organized logically and intuitively. Wireframing helps in identifying potential usability issues early and provides a clear roadmap for the subsequent stages of design.

Once the wireframe is in place, the next step is prototyping. Prototyping in Figma or any tool of choice allows you to create interactive models of your dashboard, enabling you to test and refine the design before moving into development. This step is crucial for gathering feedback and making adjustments based on user interactions. Prototyping helps in bridging the gap between concept and reality, ensuring that the final product meets user expectations and business objectives.

Designing the layout of your dashboard involves careful consideration of visual hierarchy, balance, and spacing. The layout should guide the user's eye to the most important information first, making it easy to understand at a glance. Effective use of color, typography, and whitespace can enhance readability and ensure that the dashboard is aesthetically pleasing.

Looker Studio offers different customization options for themes, layouts, and pages. By leveraging these features, you can create dashboards that are not only functional but also align with your brand identity. Custom themes allow for consistent styling, while flexible layouts enable you to organize information in a way that best suits your users' needs.

Understanding the native chart types and styles available in Looker Studio is essential for effective data visualization. Each chart type has its strengths and is suited to different types of data. Choosing the right chart for your data ensures that the information is presented clearly and effectively. Looker Studio's styling options allow you to customize charts to enhance their visual appeal and align with your overall design.

Translating your Figma designs into Looker Studio dashboards involves importing assets, setting up data connectors, and configuring interactive elements. This step ensures that your design vision is accurately reflected in the final product. Building interactive dashboards with features like filters and drill-downs enhances user engagement and provides a dynamic data exploration experience.

This section will equip you with the knowledge and tools to design and implement effective dashboards using design tools and Looker Studio. By comprehending the overall approach and finding the middle grounds where design meets data analytics, you should be able to create dashboards that not only look good but also provide valuable insights that drive informed decision-making.

Overview of Dashboard Design

> In this chapter, you will learn how to design dashboards that transform raw data into actionable insights, prioritizing user needs and usability through effective visual and interactive design techniques.

Dashboard design is the art and science of creating visual interfaces that effectively communicate data insights. A well-designed dashboard presents complex information in a clear, concise, and visually appealing manner, enabling users to make informed decisions quickly and efficiently. The principles of dashboard design are grounded in visual design fundamentals, user experience (UX) best practices, and data visualization techniques. The goal is to transform raw data into actionable insights through an intuitive and engaging visual interface.

Importance of User-centric Design

User-centric design places the needs and preferences of the end-user at the forefront of the design process. By understanding who the users are, what they need from the dashboard, and how they will interact with it, designers can create interfaces that are both functional and engaging. This approach ensures that the dashboard is not just a static display of data, but a dynamic tool that supports users in their decision-making processes.

Practical Application

To implement user-centric design and data storytelling effectively, it is crucial to follow a structured process that includes a thorough understanding of the data needed. Here are the practical steps to guide you:

User Research

Conduct interviews, surveys, and observation sessions to gather insights into user needs and preferences. Understand the specific goals of different user groups, such as executives, marketing managers, or operations staff. This initial research helps in identifying what metrics and dimensions are most relevant to each user group.

Metric and Dimension Study

Analyze and identify the key metrics and dimensions to understand the context of the data that will be included in the dashboard. This involves understanding the types of data that are most relevant to your users' objectives. For example, for a marketing manager, this might include metrics like conversion rates, customer acquisition costs, and campaign ROI. Dimensions could include customer demographics, geographical data, and time periods. This study ensures that the data visualizations are aligned with the users' decision-making needs.

Empathy Mapping

Develop empathy maps to visualize user pain points, goals, and behaviors. This helps in understanding the context in which users will interact with the dashboard and the type of insights they are seeking. Empathy maps can highlight specific user frustrations with existing data tools and what improvements they hope to see.

Persona Development

Create detailed user personas based on the insights gathered from user research and empathy mapping. Each persona should include information about the user's role, responsibilities, data needs, and preferred methods of data interaction. Personas guide design decisions by keeping the focus on the end-user throughout the design process.

Wireframing

Use wireframes to plan the layout and structure of the dashboard. This step involves sketching the overall design and placement of visual elements like charts, graphs, and tables. Wireframes should be created with the user personas in mind, ensuring that the design aligns with their needs and preferences. This is also the stage where you decide how the identified metrics and dimensions will be visually represented.

Prototyping

Develop interactive prototypes using tools like Figma. Prototyping allows you to create a working model of the dashboard, which can be tested and refined. During this phase, pay close attention to the usability of the interactive elements and the clarity of the data visualizations. Ensure that users can easily navigate through the dashboard and interact with the data in meaningful ways.

Feedback and Iteration

Continuously gather feedback from users and iterate on the design. This involves conducting usability testing sessions where real users interact with the prototype. Collect feedback on what works well and what needs improvement. Use this feedback to make iterative enhancements to the dashboard design, focusing on improving user experience and ensuring the dashboard effectively supports their decision-making processes.

Testing Visualizations

Test different types of visualizations to find the most effective ways to present the data. This may involve testing different chart types, color schemes, and layouts to see which ones are most intuitive and informative for users. Ensure that the visualizations highlight the key insights and trends identified during the metric and dimension study.

Implementation

Translate the finalized design into a working dashboard using Looker Studio. Ensure that the visualizations are accurately represented and that all interactive elements function as intended. This step involves close collaboration between designers and analysts to bring the prototype to life.

Ongoing Evaluation

After the dashboard is deployed, continue to evaluate its effectiveness. Gather user feedback on its performance and make necessary adjustments. Monitor how the dashboard is being used and identify any new requirements that may arise. This ensures the dashboard remains relevant and useful over time.

By following these steps as needed and focusing on user-centric design and data storytelling, you can create dashboards that not only present data but also drive meaningful insights and business outcomes. This not a linear structured approach that must be followed exactly step by step rather than being a guide that ultimately ensures that the final product is tailored to the needs of its users, making it a powerful tool for decision-making.

Key Considerations for Effective Dashboard Design

Designing an effective dashboard involves a careful balance of aesthetics, functionality, and user experience. Here are the key considerations to keep in mind:

Define Clear Objectives

Establish clear objectives for your dashboard. What questions is it supposed to answer? What decisions will it support? By defining these objectives upfront, you can ensure that the dashboard remains focused and relevant. Each visual element should serve a specific purpose and contribute to the overall goal of the dashboard.

Example 1: Executive Dashboard for C-Level Users

- **Objective**: Provide high-level insights for strategic decision-making.
- **Questions to Answer**: What is the overall health of the business? Are key performance indicators (KPIs) being met? What areas need immediate attention?
- **Decisions to Support**: Strategic planning, resource allocation, identifying growth opportunities.

Figure 11. Executive dashboard low-fidelity sketch

In this example, we concentrate on presenting metrics that are straightforward and cover extended periods. The aim is to minimize excessive detail in terms of time frames, metric breakdowns, or complexity of the metrics, ensuring clarity.

Example 2: Marketing Dashboard for Brand and User Experience Managers

- **Objective**: Provide detailed insights to optimize website marketing performance and user experience.
- **Questions to Answer**: How is my website performing? What is my website conversion rate? Where are the drop-off points in the conversion funnel?
- **Decisions to Support**: UX design changes to enhance user interaction and increase conversion rates.

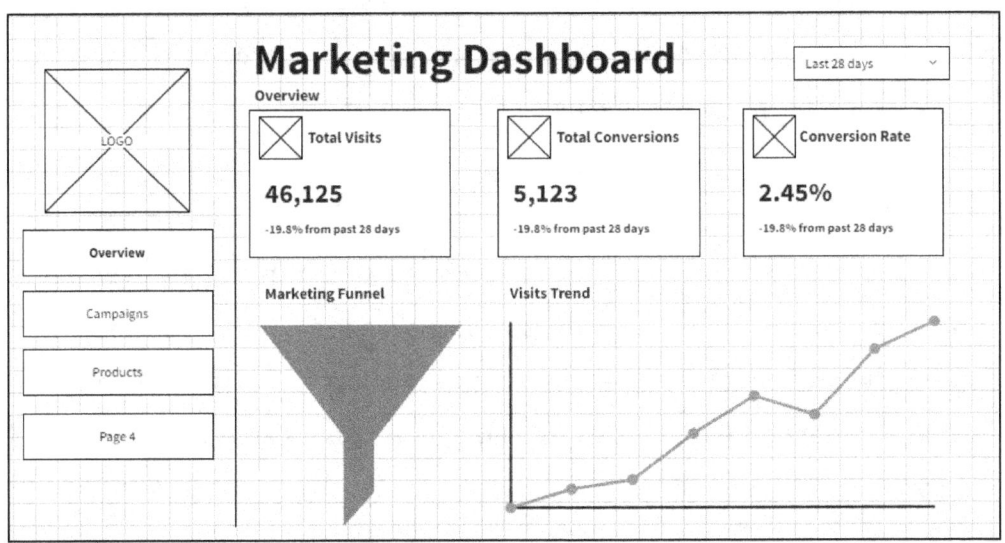

Figure 12. Marketing dashboard low-fidelity sketch

By understanding the flow through the marketing funnel and identifying trends in site visits, the team in this example can make data-driven decisions to optimize marketing strategies and improve user experience. For instance, a marketing manager could use the trend analysis to assess the impact of a recent campaign launch

Simplicity and Clarity

Strive for simplicity in your design. Avoid cluttering the dashboard with too much information or too many visual elements. Split your data into section, and different pages if needed.

Use white space effectively to create a clean and organized layout. Ensure that the most important information is easily accessible and prominently displayed. Clarity is key; users should be able to understand the data at a glance.

Consistent Design Language

Maintain a consistent design language throughout the dashboard. This includes using uniform colors, fonts, and chart types. Consistency helps users to quickly interpret the data and reduces cognitive load. It also contributes to a more professional and polished appearance.

Effective Use of Color

Use color strategically to highlight key information and differentiate between data sets. Choose color palettes that are accessible to all users. Avoid using too many colors, as this can be overwhelming and confusing. Instead, use a few complementary colors to create a visually appealing and easy-to-read dashboard.

Interactive Elements

Incorporate interactive elements such as filters, drill-downs, and hover effects to enhance user engagement. Interactive elements allow users to explore the data in more depth and customize their view based on their specific needs. However, ensure that these interactions are intuitive and do not complicate the user experience.

Data Integrity and Accuracy

Ensure that the data displayed on the dashboard is accurate and up-to-date. Regularly update the data and perform quality checks to maintain its integrity. Inaccurate or outdated data can lead to incorrect conclusions and undermine the credibility of the dashboard.

User Testing and Feedback

Conduct user testing throughout the design process to gather feedback and identify areas for improvement. Involve actual users in the testing phase to ensure that the dashboard meets their needs and expectations. Iterate on the design based on feedback to enhance usability and effectiveness.

Wireframing for Dashboard Design

Wireframing is a crucial step in the dashboard design process as mentioned earlier since it allows designers to visualize the layout and structure of the dashboard before adding detailed design elements. This stage focuses on the arrangement of components, such as charts, graphs, and filters, to ensure they effectively convey the intended information and support user interactions.

Key Considerations for Wireframing Involve:

Identifying Key Components

Start by determining the essential elements that need to be included in the dashboard based on user needs and objectives. This may include key metrics, trend analysis, and comparative data.

Arranging Components Intuitively

Organize the components in a logical and intuitive manner to facilitate easy navigation and understanding. Consider the flow of information and how users will interact with the dashboard.

Balance Visual Appeal and Functionality

While aesthetics is important, prioritize functionality and usability. Ensure that each component serves a specific purpose and contributes to the overall effectiveness of the dashboard.

Chapter Recap

- **User-centric Design**: Prioritize user needs and usability in the design process.

- **Structured Process**: Follow steps like user research, wireframing, and prototyping.

- **Clear Objectives**: Define and focus on clear dashboard goals.

- **Effective Visuals**: Use strategic color, form, and layout for clarity.

Wireframing & Prototyping with Collaborative Design Platforms (Figma)

> In this section, you will explore the essential tools and techniques for creating wireframes, the foundational step in designing effective dashboards. You will also gain insights into using Figma as a prototyping tool and how to get started with collaborative design software.

Tools and Techniques for Creating Wireframes

Wireframing is a crucial step in the design process, allowing designers to create a visual blueprint of the dashboard layout. Techniques such as sketching, low-fidelity wireframes, and digital wireframing help designers explore different layout ideas and user interactions before committing to a final design. Incorporating common dashboard elements such as charts, tables, and navigation menus into wireframes ensures that the final design meets user needs.

Tools

Designers can choose from a variety of tools for wireframing, ranging from basic pen and paper sketches to more user-friendly sketching tools like Miro or Canva, till the most advanced design tools like Adobe XD, Sketch, or Figma. Each tool offers its own set of features and complexity, allowing designers to select the one that best fits their needs and proficiency.

Techniques

Sketching is often the first step in wireframing, allowing designers to quickly draft layout ideas. Low-fidelity wireframes, created with simple shapes and placeholders, help in mapping out the basic structure and content placement.

Digital wireframing then takes these ideas into a more refined digital format, adding details and interactivity.

Exploration and Validation

Wireframing enables designers to explore various layout ideas and user interactions. By creating different versions of wireframes, designers can validate their design choices with stakeholders and potential users before investing time and resources in development.

Incorporating Dashboard Elements

During the wireframing process, it's crucial to include common dashboard elements such as charts, tables, and navigation menus. This ensures that the layout effectively presents the necessary information and supports the desired user interactions. By incorporating these elements early on, designers can ensure not only that the final design meets user needs and expectations, but essentially that it can start developing on the right foundations and that in the later iterations the usability of the dashboard will not be compromised or that the aesthetic aspect of the design will drown will transform into clutter.

Wireframing for Dashboards

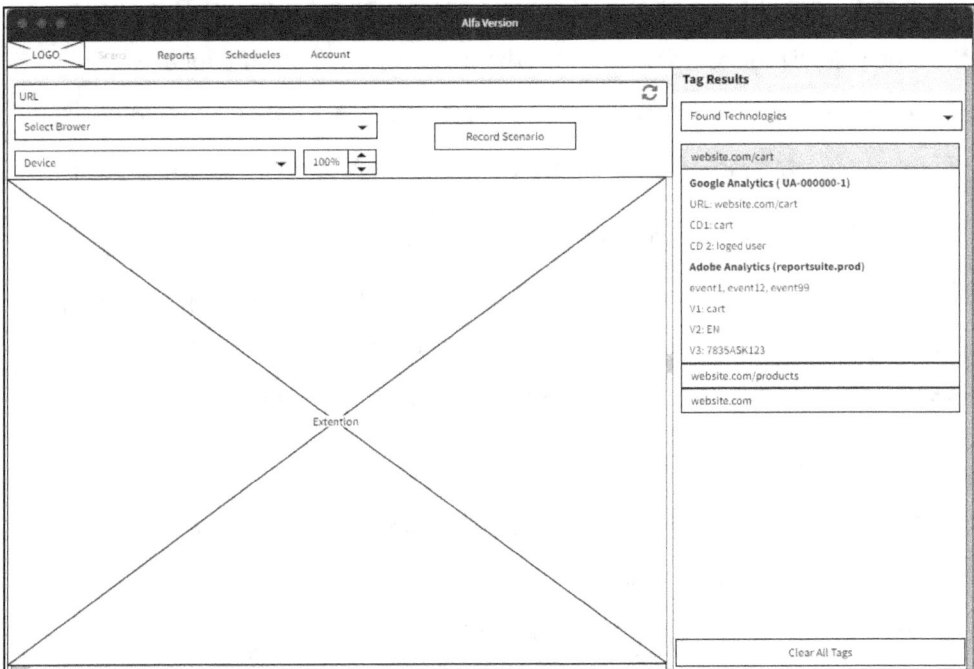

Figure 13. Wireframe example of a software UI basic sketch

When wireframing for dashboards, especially those intended for platforms like Google Looker Studio, designers should adopt a unique approach that emphasizes functionality, usability, and adaptability. Unlike traditional web or app design, dashboard wireframing requires a deeper understanding of the data being presented and the specific needs of the users interacting with it.

One key aspect of wireframing for dashboards is to start with a clear understanding of the dashboard's objectives and the target audience in relation to its functionalities. This understanding helps in determining the most relevant data visualizations and interactive elements to include. For example, an executive dashboard may prioritize high-level KPIs and trends, while a marketing dashboard may focus on campaign performance and audience segmentation.

Given Looker Studio's limitations in design customization, wireframes should focus on leveraging the platform's native chart types and styles. This ensures that the visualizations not only meet the design standards of Looker Studio but also effectively communicate the data insights. It's important to avoid overly complex layouts or interactions that may not translate well into the platform.

Since Looker Studio does not offer responsive design capabilities, wireframes should account for different screen sizes and resolutions. Designing with a responsive mindset helps ensure that the dashboard remains accessible and usable across a variety of devices, from desktops to mobile devices.

Another key consideration is the use of data visualization techniques that are both informative and visually engaging. Charts, graphs, and other visual elements should be chosen based on their ability to convey insights clearly and efficiently. Each element should serve a specific purpose and contribute to the overall narrative of the dashboard.

In summary, wireframing for dashboards in Looker Studio requires a thoughtful approach that balances functionality, data context, usability, and design constraints. By focusing on the unique requirements of the platform and the needs of the users, designers can create dashboards that are not only visually appealing but also highly effective in communicating data-driven insights.

Introduction to Figma as a prototyping tool

Figma has emerged as a leading prototyping tool for designers, offering a range of features that streamline the design process and facilitate collaboration. As a web-based platform, Figma allows multiple users to work on the same project simultaneously, making it ideal for team collaboration and remote work. Its intuitive interface and robust set of tools make it a popular choice for creating interactive prototypes for dashboards, websites, and mobile apps.

One of the key advantages of Figma is its versatility. It allows designers to create wireframes, high-fidelity mockups, and interactive prototypes all within the same platform. This integrated approach helps maintain consistency across the design process and ensures a seamless transition from concept to final product.

Figma's prototyping capabilities enable designers to create interactive experiences that closely mimic the final product's functionality. Designers can create clickable prototypes with interactive elements such as buttons, dropdowns, and metric sliders, making it easy to test user interactions and gather feedback early in the design process.

Another notable feature of Figma is its component-based design system. Designers can create reusable components such as buttons, navigation bars, and cards, which can be easily replicated and edited throughout the design. This approach not only speeds up the design process but also ensures consistency across the dashboard or application.

Figma also offers robust collaboration features, allowing designers to share prototypes with team members or stakeholders for feedback. Comments can be added directly to the design, facilitating communication and streamlining the feedback loop.

Prototyping with Figma or Other Collaborative Design Software: Getting Started

Before diving into the specifics of designing your dashboard prototype, it's important to ensure you're familiar with the basics of using Figma or any other similar tool. If you're new to Figma, it's recommended to go through some basic tutorials or guides to familiarize yourself with the interface and tools. Below are the main areas that will be essential in prototyping processes:

- Creating a New Project in Figma

- Navigating the Canvas
- Organizing Your Layers
- Exporting Assets & Files
- Overview of the Figma Tools
- Setting Up Your Dashboard Artboard
- Styling Your Elements
- Commenting and Sharing
- Connecting Frames to Prototype
- Previewing Your Prototype

By familiarizing yourself with these basics, you'll be ready to start designing your dashboard prototype in Figma. Remember, the key to effective prototyping is to iterate and gather feedback from users to refine your design.

Chapter Recap

- **Wireframing Tools**: From basic sketches to advanced software, familiarize yourself with tools your organization is using or adopt suitable ones like Adobe XD, Sketch, and Figma.

- **Techniques**: Steps from initial sketches to low-fidelity and detailed digital wireframes.

- **Exploration and Validation**: Experiment with layouts and validate design choices early.

- **Essential Elements**: Include charts, tables, and navigation in your wireframes for comprehensive design.

- **Dashboard-Specific Wireframing**: Focus on functionality and adaptability, especially for platforms like Looker Studio.

- **Figma Introduction**: Learn Figma's collaborative features, versatility, and component-based design system.

- **Starting with Figma or your tool of choice**: Set up and create your first interactive prototypes in your dashboard design process.

Designing Dashboard Layouts

> In this chapter, you will discover key principles for designing effective dashboard layouts, recognize common pitfalls in ineffective designs, and learn actionable steps to create user-friendly and visually appealing dashboards.

Principles of Layout Design for Dashboards

Designing an effective dashboard layout requires careful consideration of various principles to ensure that the dashboard is not only visually appealing but also functional and user-friendly. Here are key principles to keep in mind:

Hierarchy

Establish a clear hierarchy of information, with the most important and relevant data presented prominently. Use size, color, and placement to guide the user's attention.

Consistency

Maintain consistency in the layout, typography, and color scheme throughout the dashboard to create a cohesive and professional look. Consistency helps users navigate the dashboard more easily.

Whitespace

Use whitespace or blank areas strategically to separate different sections and elements, making the dashboard more visually appealing and easier to scan. Whitespace can also help draw attention to important data points.

Alignment

Ensure that elements are aligned properly to create a sense of order and organization. Misaligned elements can make the dashboard appear cluttered and confusing.

Balance

Achieve visual balance by distributing elements evenly throughout the dashboard. Avoid overcrowding one area while leaving other areas empty.

Contrast

Use contrast to highlight important data and create visual interest. Contrast can be achieved through color, size, or style differences.

Typography

Choose legible fonts and font sizes for text elements. Use typography to differentiate between different types of information, such as headings, labels, and data points.

Examples of Ineffective Dashboard Layouts

Ineffective dashboard layouts can hinder the user experience, making it challenging for viewers to extract valuable insights from the data presented. These layouts often suffer from cluttered designs, lack of hierarchy, and poor use of visualizations, among other issues.

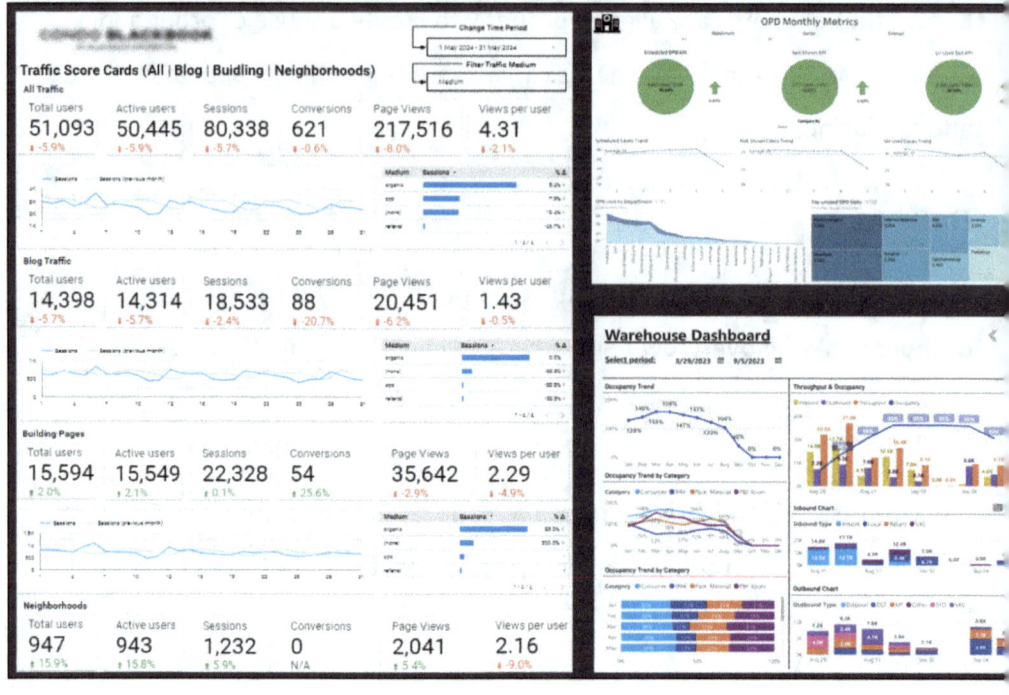

Figure 14. Visual examples of ineffective layouts

Cluttered Design

The dashboard shown appears cluttered, with too much information crammed into a small space. This makes it difficult for users to focus on key metrics and find the information they need.

Lack of Hierarchy

The layout lacks a clear hierarchy, making it challenging for users to prioritize information. Important metrics are not highlighted, leading to confusion.

Inconsistent Design

Inconsistencies in color, typography, and spacing make the dashboard look disjointed and unprofessional. This inconsistency can also affect readability.

Poor Use of Visualizations

Visualizations are either missing or poorly designed, making it hard to interpret the data. Charts and graphs are cluttered or unclear, failing to communicate the intended message.

Complex Navigation

The dashboard has complex navigation menus or structures, making it difficult for users to navigate between different sections. This complexity can frustrate users and hinder their ability to find information quickly.

Chapter Recap

- **Prioritize Information**: Use hierarchy to guide users' attention.
- **Be Consistent**: Uniform layout, typography, and color scheme.
- **Utilize Whitespace**: Separate sections and enhance visual appeal.
- **Align Elements**: Ensure proper alignment for order and clarity.
- **Balance Visuals**: Distribute elements evenly to avoid clutter.
- **Use Contrast**: Highlight key data with color, size, or style differences.
- **Choose Legible Fonts**: Clear fonts and sizes for readability.
- **Avoid Clutter**: Don't overload with too much information.
- **Highlight Important Data**: Ensure clear hierarchy.
- **Maintain Consistency**: Uniform design elements for readability.
- **Improve Visuals**: Clear, effective charts and graphs.
- **Simplify Navigation**: Easy and intuitive user navigation.

Expectation Setting: Understanding Looker Studio Design & Styling

> In this chapter, you will explore Looker Studio's design and styling capabilities, understand its limitations, and learn techniques to create effective dashboards despite these constraints.

Capabilities

When designing dashboards in Looker Studio, it is essential to set realistic expectations regarding the platform's design and styling capabilities. Looker Studio offers various tools to create effective dashboards, but it also has several limitations that designers should be aware of to maximize the platform's potential.

Design and Styling Capabilities

Looker Studio is not a collaborative design tool like Figma, Adobe XD, or Sketch. Instead, it offers features similar to those found in Google Slides or Microsoft PowerPoint. While it can produce visually appealing dashboards, it lacks some of the advanced design capabilities of dedicated design software. Here are some key points to consider:

Basic Design Tools

Shape Creation

Looker Studio provides basic tools for creating shapes such as lines, rectangles, and circles. However, the ability to create custom shapes is limited. Designers often rely on external image files to introduce more complex shapes.

Text and Typography

The platform supports adding and formatting text, including font selection, size adjustments, and color settings. However, advanced typography controls are limited compared to dedicated design tools.

Styling Options

Color and Gradients

Styling includes setting colors with some gradient options. While basic color customization is straightforward, the platform does not support advanced color management features like color palettes or custom gradient creation.

Borders and Shadows

Looker Studio allows setting borders with adjustable radius, weight, and style (solid, dashed, double, or dotted). Drop shadows can be applied, but without adjustable settings, limiting their customization.

Transparency and Backgrounds

Transparency Settings

Designers can adjust the transparency of shapes and images, enabling layering effects and visual hierarchy.

Background Effects

Background styling is limited to basic color and gradient settings. The platform does not support advanced background effects or custom CSS for detailed styling.

Grids and Guides

Alignment Tools

The platform allows for setting grids and guides, which aid in aligning elements. These tools are crucial for maintaining consistent spacing and alignment across the dashboard.

Snapping to the grid: Elements can snap to grids and guides, ensuring that they are placed accurately. This feature helps maintain a clean and organized layout.

Image Imports

Image Handling

It is possible to import image files into Looker Studio to enhance the visual appeal of dashboards. However, large image files can slow down the loading process, affecting performance.

Image Positioning

Imported images can be resized and positioned, but the platform does not support advanced image editing capabilities. Designers should prepare images in external software before importing them into Looker Studio.

Limitations and Workarounds

Understanding the limitations of Looker Studio is crucial for creating effective dashboards. Here are some of the main limitations and how to work around them:

Layer Management

Lack of Layer Hierarchy

Looker Studio does not support multi-layer element management with a hierarchy view. This can make it challenging to manage and order grouped elements, especially in complex dashboards. Designers need to manually adjust the arrangement of elements, which can become cumbersome as the complexity of the dashboard increases.

Element Grouping

Grouping elements is possible, but the lack of a layer list or hierarchy view makes it difficult to manage and reorder groups. Designers should use consistent naming conventions and grouping practices to keep track of elements.

Limited Shape Creation

Basic Shapes Only

Beyond basic shapes (lines, rectangles, circles), there is no capability to create custom shapes or vectors. Designers must rely on external image files to introduce more complex shapes. This can limit the flexibility of design elements within the dashboard.

External Tools

To create custom shapes, designers should use external design tools like Adobe Illustrator or Figma and import the shapes as images into Looker Studio.

Resizing and Precision

Drag-Based Resizing

Resizing elements is done by dragging, which lacks the precision of numeric input for dimensions. This can make it difficult to achieve exact sizes and placements. Designers should use grids and guides to assist with alignment and spacing.

Positioning Constraints

Accurate positioning of elements can be challenging without numeric input. Designers should leverage snapping features and consistent spacing guidelines to maintain order.

Styling Restrictions

No Advanced Styling

Advanced styling options such as CSS or JavaScript customization are not available. Designers should focus on the native styling features and explore creative ways to achieve the desired look within these limitations.

Combining Chart Types

Complex Visualizations

To achieve complex visualizations, designers might need to combine multiple chart types. For example, to create a custom scorecard with a sparkline in a different sizing or formatting than the default scorecard layout, one would need to use a combination of a container, title, metric, and trendline. This approach, however, can quickly hit the platform's limit of 50 charts per page.

Widgets Limit

Looker Studio allows a maximum of 50 charts on a single page. Designers must be mindful of this limit and plan their dashboards accordingly. Combining chart types should be done judiciously to avoid hitting this constraint.

Lack of Animations

Static Visuals

Looker Studio does not support animations, which limits the ability to create dynamic and engaging transitions within dashboards. Designers must rely on static visuals and interactive elements to guide users through the data.

Focus on Interactivity

To compensate for the lack of animations, designers should focus on creating interactive elements such as filters, drill-downs, and hyperlinks to enhance user engagement.

Interactive Elements

Hyperlinks and Navigation

It is possible to create hyperlinks within the dashboard, adding some level of interactivity. This can be useful for guiding users through different parts of the report or linking to external resources.

User Flow Design

Designing a clear user flow with interactive elements helps users navigate the dashboard efficiently. Hyperlinks, buttons, and navigation menus should be used strategically to enhance the user experience.

By understanding these capabilities and limitations, designers can better plan their dashboard projects in Looker Studio. Leveraging the available tools effectively while being mindful of the constraints can lead to well-designed, functional dashboards that meet user needs without overcomplicating the design process. Effective use of grids, guides, and basic design tools, along with creative problem-solving, can help overcome the limitations and produce professional-looking dashboards.

Chapter Recap

- **Understand Basic Tools**: Utilize Looker Studio's basic shape creation and text formatting options.

- **Apply Basic Styling**: Use grids, guides, basic color settings, borders, and transparency for design consistency.

- **Optimize Layout**: Maintain hierarchy, consistency, whitespace, alignment, balance, and contrast.

- **Incorporate Interactivity**: Add hyperlinks and interactive elements like filters and drill-downs.

- **Navigate Limitations**: Manage layers manually, combine chart types within the 50-chart limit, and focus on static visuals due to lack of animation support.

Best Practices for Designing and Organizing Pages in Looker Studio

> In this chapter you will learn about dashboards design approach according to a common device screen size, create effective navigation, and design layouts that enhance user experience while adhering to Looker Studio's capabilities and limitations.

Designing and organizing pages in Looker Studio requires careful planning and understanding of the platform's capabilities and limitations. The following best practices help create effective and user-friendly dashboards.

Device Optimization and Canvas Size

1. Non-Responsive Design

Looker Studio dashboards do not automatically adjust to different screen sizes. Therefore, dashboards should be designed specifically for desktop use. Nothing prevents designers or analysis to design for mobile, however it is important to note that the mobile user experience is generally poor due to difficulties in interacting with elements like drop-down menus and drill-down tables.

2. Fit to Width or Actual Size Display Mode

Dashboards can be configured to either fit the browser's width or display at a static actual size. This choice depends on the desired user experience and how the dashboard will be viewed.

Selecting the right canvas size is critical. In case of fitting to actual size, the width of the dashboard will keep adjusting according to the browser width. The only downside to this setting is that if the screen is extra wide, the dashboard will adjust, what might show the dashboard elements in an extra-large format in addition to the need to scroll down due to the adapted ratio.

While in the case setting an actual size with a specific width, when the browser window's width is relatively smaller, a horizontal scroll will be there to navigate to the parts of the dashboard that does not fit into the screen.

Usually setting the size to fit to width is a good practice to guarantee a fit to screen display, with a minor risk of displaying huge elements in case of extra-wide screens. The choice to use either of the available options depends on the final users of the dashboard. If it is addressed to generic audiences without the ability to predict what screen sizes they might be using, then it is safe to assume that fitting to width is a good option, while setting an actual size can be a better option if the dashboard is addressed to an internal office team for example.

3. Dashboard Width and Height

Either way, it is possible to choose from a list of standard sizes such as:

- US letter (4:3) – Portrait
- US letter (4:3) – Landscape
- Screen (16:9) – Landscape
- Or setting a custom size for width and height in pixels

Looker Studio Header, Pagination, and Main Layout

Header Visibility

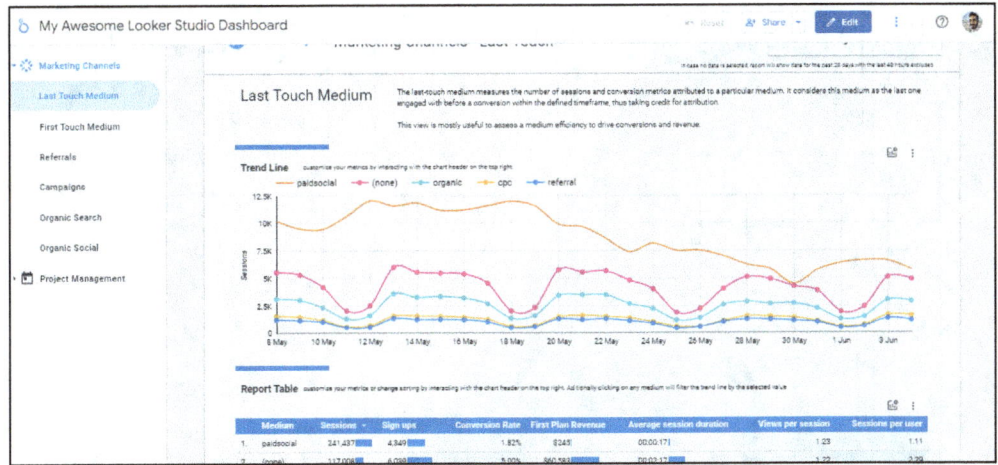

Figure 15. Looker Studio dashboard example with a visible header

The Looker Studio header includes the dashboard's main name, sharing settings, editing options, presenting, and refreshing buttons. It can be configured in three ways: initially hidden, auto-hide, or always show.

For non-technical users who primarily read data, hide the header to provide a cleaner view.

For users who frequently interact with filters, manage users, or need to edit, download, or refresh the dashboard often, keep the header always visible.

Pagination Choices: Do You Need Pagination?

Single-page Dashboards

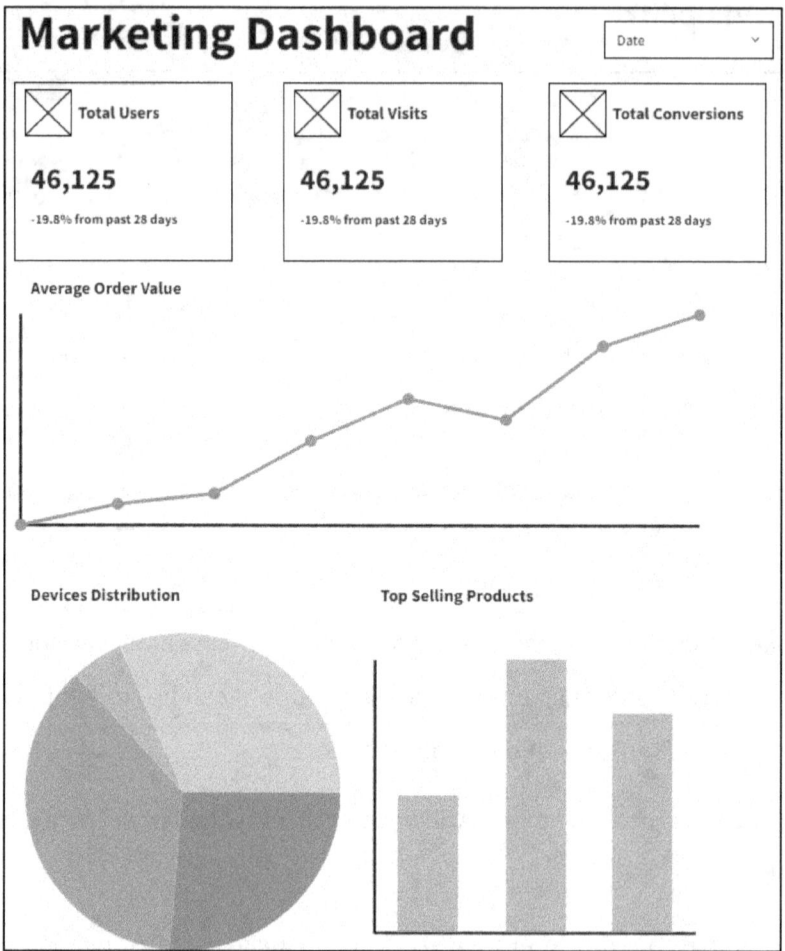

Figure 16. Low-fidelity sketch of a single page dashboard without any navigation menu

For single-page dashboards, pagination is unnecessary can be completely set to hidden, but remember the 50-widget limit per page.

With a maximum of 50 charts per page, designers need to be strategic about combining chart types to avoid hitting this limit. Complex visualizations might require creative solutions to fit within this constraint.

Multi-page Dashboards

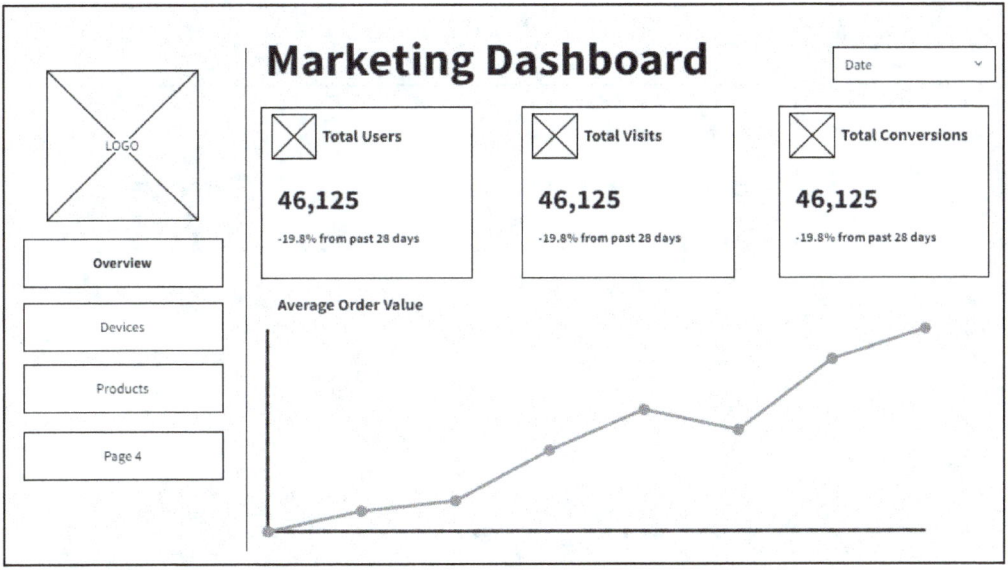

Figure 17. Low-fidelity sketch of a single page dashboard with a custom left-side navigation menu

For multi-page dashboards, decide whether to use Looker Studio's built-in pagination and page navigation or create a custom design for navigating across pages. Custom page arrangement within an integrated design will be covered next.

Default Page Navigation Menu

1. Navigation Menu Types:

Hidden: No page navigation is shown.

Top Left Arrows: Shows arrows for navigating backward and forward through pages. Clicking in the middle reveals a left-side layer menu with the page list, which can be hidden by clicking again.

Figure 18. Looker Studio dashboard header with page navigation arrows

Top Tabs: Displays all pages as tabs in a top bar above the dashboard and below the header.

Figure 19. Looker Studio dashboard with a native top side navigation menu

Left Side Menu: Can be fully expanded to show icons and page names or collapsed to show only numbers.

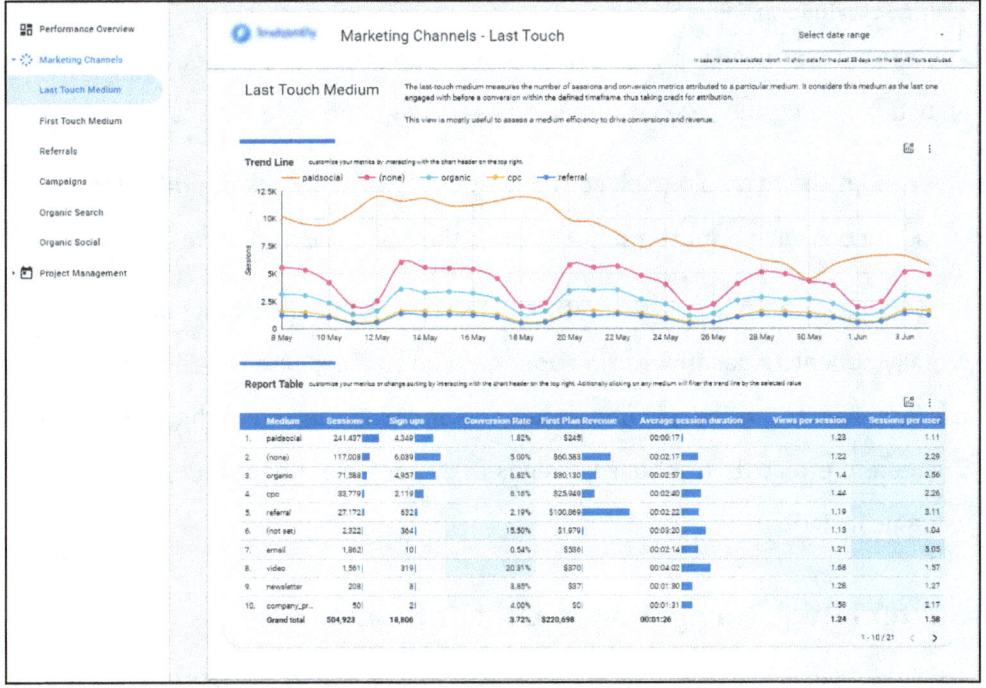

Figure 20. Looker Studio dashboard with a native left side navigation menu

2. Managing Pages and Menus:

Navigate to Page > Manage Pages to manage menu and page settings. Here, you can:

- Create headers that act as titles.
- Create or delete pages
- Rename pages and sections (names will appear in the navigation menu where applicable).
- Create sections that act as page group containers that appear as folding menus in left-side view and dropdown menus in tab view.
- Add dividers to separate pages or sections.
- Choose icons for pages or sections from approximately 70 provided options.
- Change the order of pages or sections.

3. Page Navigation Style:

You can customize the navigation style by editing the current theme layout and adjusting settings under Edit theme > Page navigation style. You can:

- Set the text color, selected text color, font, and background color.
- Icons will adopt the same color as the text (selected or not).

By working with the available features, designers can create functional and visually appealing dashboards in Looker Studio to a big extent. While the platform has its limitations, understanding and working within these constraints can lead to effective dashboard designs that meet user needs and provide valuable insights.

Custom Page Navigation in Looker Studio

Creating a custom page navigation menu in Looker Studio allows designers to bypass some of the platform's limitations and tailor the navigation experience to meet specific design requirements.

Understanding Menu Items and Levels

Before diving into the design, it is crucial to plan the basic structure of your menu. Determine the number of menu items and levels required. This planning phase ensures that your design accommodates the navigation needs without cluttering the interface.

Canvas Size Considerations & Menu Formats

Horizontal Menus: There are no strict requirements for page heights since menu components are positioned at the top. This flexibility allows for a clean and consistent look across different pages.

Side Menus: When designing side menus, consider the page height to maintain visual balance. Ensure that the menu aligns well with the content area and does not create unnecessary space adjustments between pages.

Using Available Shapes and Buttons

You can use Looker Studio's built-in shapes and buttons to construct simple and effective menu designs. Available shapes include lines, rectangles, and circles, which can be combined creatively to form menu components.

Importing Custom Visuals

For a more polished and branded look, you can design custom visuals using external graphic design tools and import them as images. This approach allows for more flexibility in design but requires consideration of image sizes to avoid slow loading times.

Making Menu Items Report-Level

To ensure that menu items appear consistently across all pages, right-click each menu component and select "Make report-level." This action sets the item to appear on every page of the report and ensures that any changes made to the menu are reflected universally. Report-level items are marked with violet borders when selected, distinguishing them from page-specific elements that have blue borders.

Highlighting the Active Page

To enhance the user experience, it is essential to highlight the currently active page. This can be achieved by adding a single visual element, such as a different color or an indicator, to the active menu item. This visual cue helps users quickly identify their current location within the dashboard. Unlike the main menu items, these indicators should be added to each specific page rather than as a report-level component.

Linking Menu Items to Pages

After finalizing the menu design and layout, the next step is to bring the menu to life by creating hyperlinks. Each menu button should be linked to its corresponding page within the report. This functionality enables seamless navigation between different sections of the dashboard.

To summarize, custom page navigation in Looker Studio involves:

- Planning the menu structure and levels.
- Designing the layout using built-in shapes or custom visuals.
- Setting menu items as report-level elements for consistency.
- Highlighting the active page for better user experience.
- Linking menu buttons to their respective pages to enable navigation.
- By following these steps, you can create a custom navigation system that enhances the usability and aesthetic appeal of your Looker Studio dashboards.

Main Layout and Component Design in Looker Studio

Flexibility in Managing Space and Components

Effective layout design is essential in creating intuitive and visually appealing dashboards. Google Looker Studio offers considerable flexibility in managing space, sizes, backgrounds, and the positioning of components within the reporting space. This flexibility allows designers to optimize the visual hierarchy and user experience of their dashboards.

A well-structured layout enhances usability and ensures that key information is easily accessible. By thoughtfully arranging components, designers can guide users through the data, making it easier to understand and interpret the information presented.

Looker Studio enables designers to float elements freely, providing the freedom to create custom and dynamic layouts. This flexibility is particularly useful for tailoring dashboards to specific needs and preferences, ensuring that all necessary information is presented in a coherent and organized manner.

After completing the main layout for the menu, it's time to continue structuring the dashboard space. This involves integrating various fixed components and interactive elements that will remain consistent across all pages, thereby providing a unified and seamless user experience.

Structuring the Main Layout with Fixed Components

After finalizing the navigation menu, the next step is to structure the dashboard space by integrating fixed components at a report level. These components provide consistency across all pages and enhance the overall user experience. Key fixed components to consider include:

- **Time Frame Controllers**: These allow users to adjust the time period for the data displayed in the dashboard. Placing them in a consistent location across all pages ensures easy access and usability.

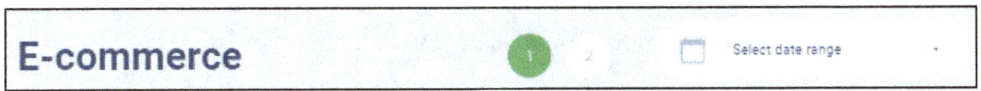

Figure 21. Time range drop down controller

- **Drop-Down Filters**: Like time frame controllers, drop-down filters should be placed consistently to allow users to interact with the data seamlessly. These filters can include dimensions such as geography, product categories, or user segments.

Figure 22. Dimensions drop down filters

- **Standardized Titles and Headings**: Consistent placement of titles and headings across the dashboard helps maintain a clear visual hierarchy and improves readability. Typically, these are placed at the top of the dashboard or sections.
- **Branding Elements**: Incorporating branding elements such as logos, color schemes, and fonts at a report level reinforces brand identity and ensures a cohesive look and feel.

Figure 23. Top-left corner dashboard logo

By making these components "report-level," you ensure that any changes made to them will be reflected across all pages. This saves time and effort and ensures consistency throughout the dashboard.

Structuring the main layout with these fixed components provides a strong foundation for the dashboard, making it easier to add and organize the dynamic content and interactive elements that will populate the rest of the space.

Designing Main Components for Effective Layout
With the main layout and fixed components in place, the focus shifts to designing the main components that will fill the dashboard space. This step involves understanding the grid system, distributing chart components effectively, and ensuring visual balance and clarity. Here are key considerations for this stage:

Google Looker Studio offers a flexible grid system that allows precise placement and sizing of components. To effectively use the grid:

Click on "Theme and layout" > "LAYOUT" > Adjust the grid settings and choose if you want to snap elements to the grid (or to smart guides).

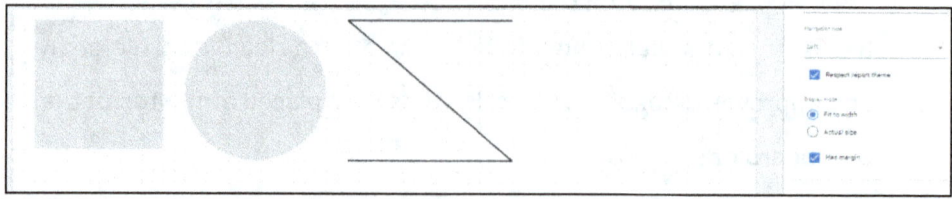

Figure 24. Basic shapes and lines on a dashboard canvas grid

- **Align Components**: Ensure that all elements are aligned according to the grid to maintain a neat and organized appearance.
- **Consistent Spacing**: Use consistent spacing between elements to create a balanced and visually appealing layout. This can be achieved by using the grid to define uniform margins and padding.

Proper distribution of chart components is crucial for an effective dashboard layout. Consider the following:

- **Hierarchy of Information**: Place the most critical information and key metrics in prominent positions, usually at the top or center of the dashboard. Less critical information can be placed further down or in less prominent areas.
- **Grouping Related Data**: Group related charts and components together to help users quickly find and compare relevant information. For example, place all sales-related charts in one section and all customer-related charts in another.
- **Visual Balance**: Ensure that the layout is visually balanced. Avoid overcrowding one area with too many components while leaving other areas sparse. Distribute the components evenly across the available space.

Correct sizing of components is essential for readability and usability:

- **Optimal Size**: Ensure that each component is large enough to be easily readable but not so large that it dominates the space and overshadows other components.
- **Responsive Sizing**: While Google Looker Studio does not support responsive design, you can create a layout that works well on the intended display device. Typically, this involves setting a fixed width and height that fit within the screen dimensions of the target device.

- **Consistent Dimensions**: Use consistent dimensions for similar types of components to maintain a cohesive look. For instance, all bar charts should have the same width and height, as should all tables and scorecards.

Consistency in layout helps users navigate and understand the dashboard more efficiently. To achieve this:

- **Standardize Component Placement**: Decide on fixed positions for common elements, such as filters, legends, and navigation menus, across all dashboards.
- **Uniform Spacing and Margins**: Use consistent spacing and margins to create a balanced and organized appearance. This includes maintaining uniform distances between components and edges of the dashboard.
- **Consistent Chart Styles**: Apply the same styling to similar types of charts. For example, if you use a specific style for bar charts (e.g., rounded edges, specific colors), ensure all bar charts across your dashboards follow this style.

By carefully considering these aspects, you can create a dashboard layout that is not only aesthetically pleasing but also highly functional and user-friendly. This structured approach ensures that all elements are logically placed, easy to interpret, and contribute to the overall effectiveness of the dashboard.

Enhancing Visual Consistency and Branding Dashboards

Enhancing visual consistency and incorporating branding elements are key aspects of creating professional and recognizable dashboards. This section will focus on strategies and techniques to achieve these goals without overlapping with previously discussed content.

Establish a Visual Style Guide

Creating a visual style guide ensures that all elements of the dashboard adhere to a consistent look and feel. This guide should include:

- **Color Palette**: Define a color palette that aligns with your brand's colors. Stick to a limited number of colors to maintain a clean and professional appearance.
- **Typography**: Choose a consistent set of fonts for all text elements. Use different font sizes and weights to create a clear hierarchy of information.
- **Icons and Imagery**: Select a consistent style for icons and images that match your brand's visual identity.

Use Brand Assets

Incorporating brand assets into your dashboard helps reinforce brand recognition and trust. Consider the following:

- **Logos**: Include your company's logo in a prominent position, such as the top-left corner of the dashboard. Ensure it is of high quality and appropriately sized.
- **Brand Colors**: Apply brand colors to various elements, such as charts, headings, and backgrounds, to create a cohesive visual experience. Looker Studio allows the setting of 10 chart colors to be used in the visualizations, that can be inspired from brand main colors and their variations for visual consistency
- **Branded Templates**: Create and use branded templates for common dashboard components, such as headers, footers, and filters. This not only saves time but also ensures consistency across different dashboard pages.

Apply Branding to Interactive Elements

Interactive elements, such as filters and buttons, should also reflect your brand's visual identity:

Button Styles: Use branded colors and fonts for buttons. Ensure buttons are clearly distinguishable as interactive elements by using appropriate styling, such as shadows or borders.

Filter Design: Style filters to match the overall dashboard design. For instance, use branded colors for dropdown menus and slider handles.

Use Custom Backgrounds and Borders

Custom backgrounds and borders can add a professional touch to your dashboards:

- **Backgrounds**: Apply subtle branded backgrounds, such as gradients or patterns, to add depth without overwhelming the data. Ensure the background does not distract from the content.
- **Borders and Shadows**: Use borders and shadows to highlight key elements and create a sense of hierarchy. For instance, use borders to separate different sections of the dashboard and shadows to give depth to charts and cards.

Looker Studio Theme Settings

> In this chapter your will learn to efficiently set up and apply themes in Looker Studio to ensure visual coherence and enhance the appeal of your reports.

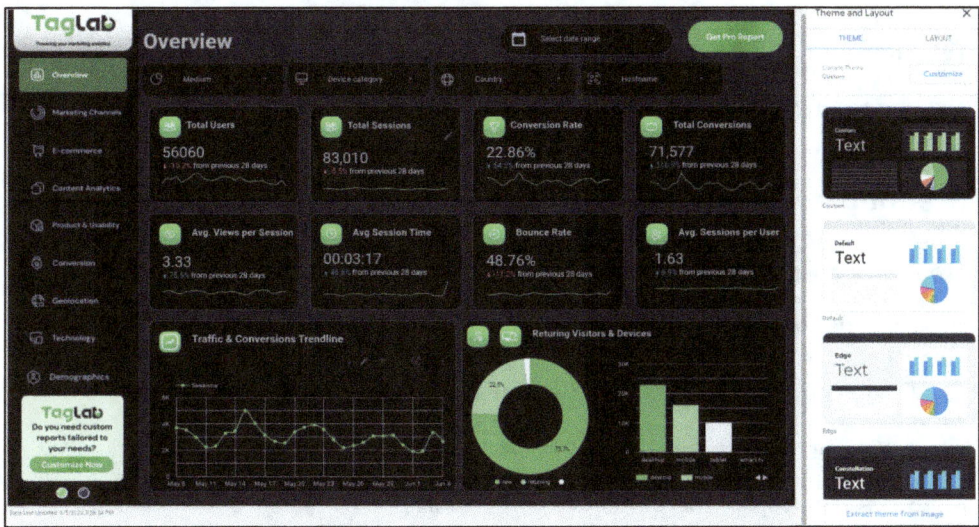

Figure 25. Custom made dark theme

Setting up theme settings early when starting a project in Looker Studio can save a significant amount of time. By establishing a consistent and visually appealing theme from the beginning, all later elements and charts created will automatically be styled as desired, ensuring coherence and attractiveness across the entire report.

Themes Overview

Themes in Looker Studio are predefined color and style combinations that can be applied to your reports. They include settings for charts, tables, background color, and text, making it easy to ensure your reports are visually cohesive. Each new report starts with a default theme, designed to be attractive and accessible, including to viewers with color blindness.

Applying a Theme

To apply a theme:

1. Edit the report.
2. In the toolbar, click on Theme and layout.
3. In the THEME tab, click the theme that you want to apply.

This simple process instantly updates the style settings of your report elements, aligning them with the chosen theme.

Creating a Custom Theme

Creating a custom theme involves modifying the current theme settings. To create a custom theme:

1. Sign in to Looker Studio and edit your report.
2. In the toolbar, click on Theme and layout.
3. At the top of the panel, click Customize.
4. Use the settings in the Edit theme panel to customize the theme.

The Edit theme panel allows you to personalize:

- **Primary styles**: Report background, text style, component background and border, border shadow.
- **Accent styles**: Font color and family for text accents, including table headers and control headers.
- **Textbox styles**: Background color, font color and family, border visibility.
- **Data styles**: Chart palette, chart styling defaults, dimension values colors, text contrast, component grid style, positive and negative change colors, chart header.

Extracting a Theme from an Image

You can generate a custom theme based on the colors in an image, ensuring that your report's color scheme aligns perfectly with your branding. To extract a theme from an image:

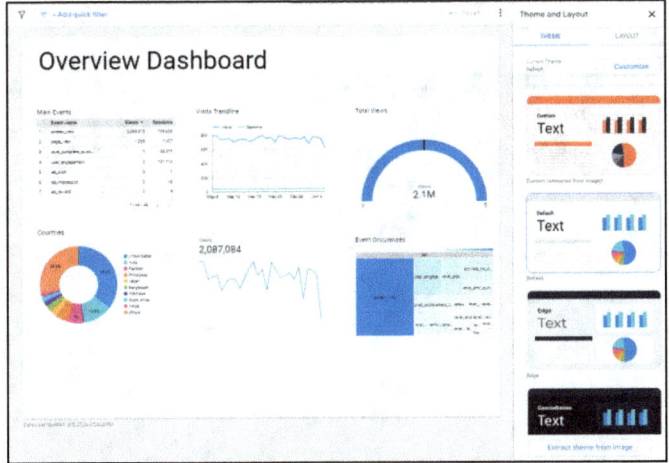

Figure 26. Setting a custom theme Step 1

1. Sign in to Looker Studio and edit your report.
2. Right-click an image in your report and select Extract theme from image.

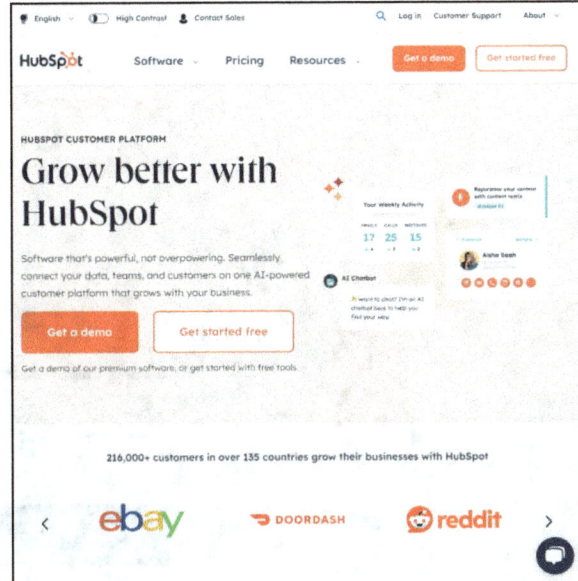

Figure 27. Setting a custom theme Step 2

3. Upload your image

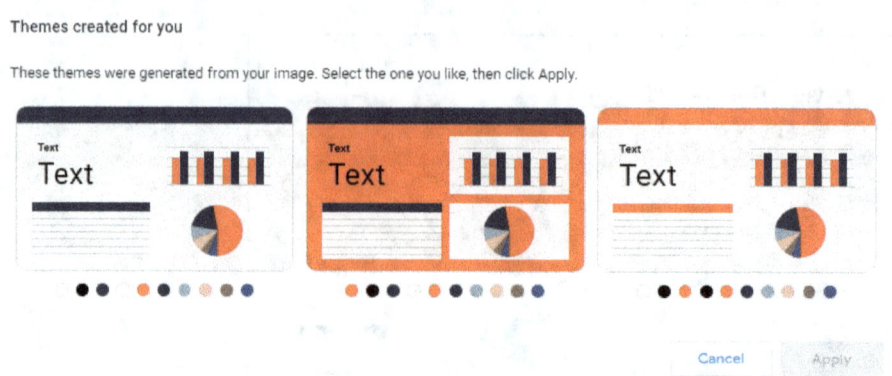

Figure 28. Setting a custom theme Step 3

Looker Studio will generate several themes from the colors in the selected image. Choose one, then click Apply. The theme will reflect on your page layout and charts.

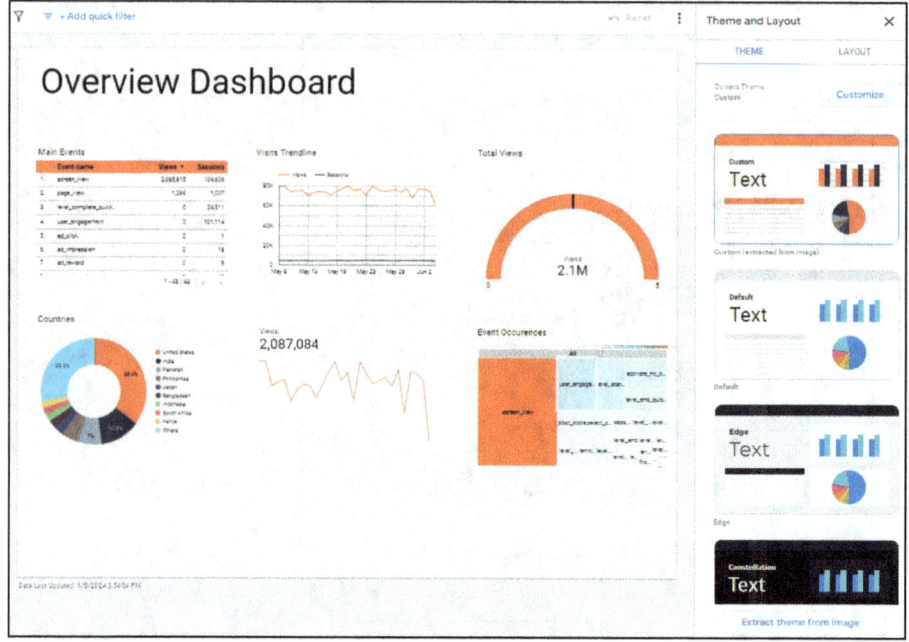

Figure 29. Setting a custom theme Step 4

Customizing Looker Studio's Native Chart Types & Visualizations

> Explore the common styling settings in Looker Studio to enhance the visual appeal and functionality of your dashboards, making your data presentations clear and engaging.

Figure 30. Chart type selection

When it comes to data visualization, selecting the appropriate chart type is crucial for effectively communicating insights and trends. Google Looker Studio offers a variety of native chart types that can be tailored to fit different data presentation needs. Understanding these chart types, along with their customization options, is essential for creating visually appealing and informative dashboards. This section will provide an overview of the native chart types available in Looker Studio and offer tips for customizing each type to enhance your dashboard's design and functionality.

By mastering the native chart types customization options, you can create dashboards that are not only functional but also visually engaging. This will help you better convey your data stories and support data-driven decision-making processes.

In this section we will go through the main visualization types, their variations, use cases, and design options.

Common Styling Settings

By default, chart styles are either inherited from the theme. In this section, we will explore the fundamental styling settings available in Google Looker Studio that apply across various chart types. Understanding these common styling options is essential for creating visually appealing and effective data visualizations. These settings provide a foundation for customizing your charts, allowing you to maintain a consistent design aesthetic and improve the clarity of your data presentations. Later in this guide, we will delve into specific styling techniques for each chart type, but first, let's establish a solid understanding of the universal styling tools at your disposal.

Title

If you select the Show title checkbox, you can add a title and customize its appearance and placement position or alignment on the chart.

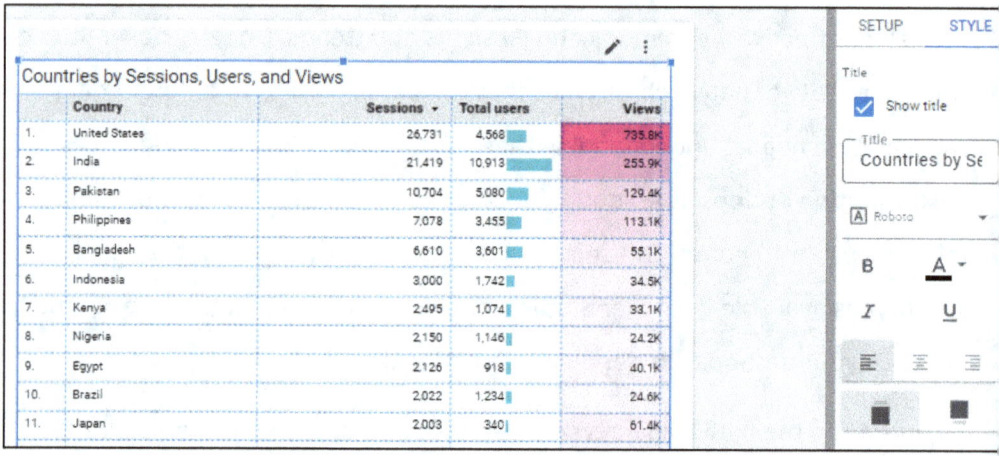

Figure 31. Table chart style adjustment

Chart header

The chart header lets viewers perform various actions on the chart, such as exporting the data, drilling up or down, changing metrics, or sorting the chart. Chart header options are as follows:

- **Show on hover (default):** Three vertical dots appear when you mouse over the chart header. Click these to access the header options.
- **Always show:** The header options always appear.
- **Do not show:** The header options never appear. Note that report viewers can always access the options by right-clicking the chart.

A good practice is to hide chart headers in case it is not believed that users will be using the available functions. Otherwise in case of drilling up or down, or metric controls (optional metrics & metric sliders), then it is advised to keep the headers on. Showing headers on hover can be used when the dashboard users have more advanced knowledge in looker studio and are aware of such options. Make sure the the proper set up of mentioned header options is correctly configured in the SETUP tab of the chart.

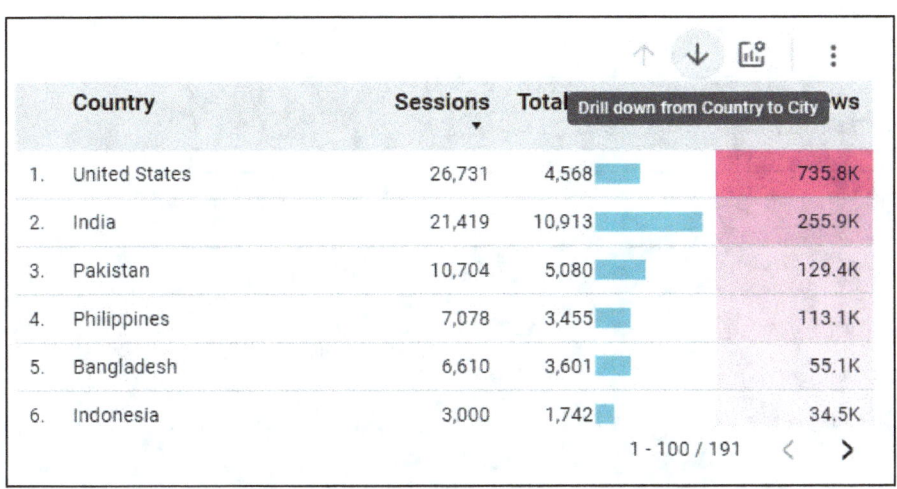

Figure 32. Table chart with dimension drill down arrows shown in the table header

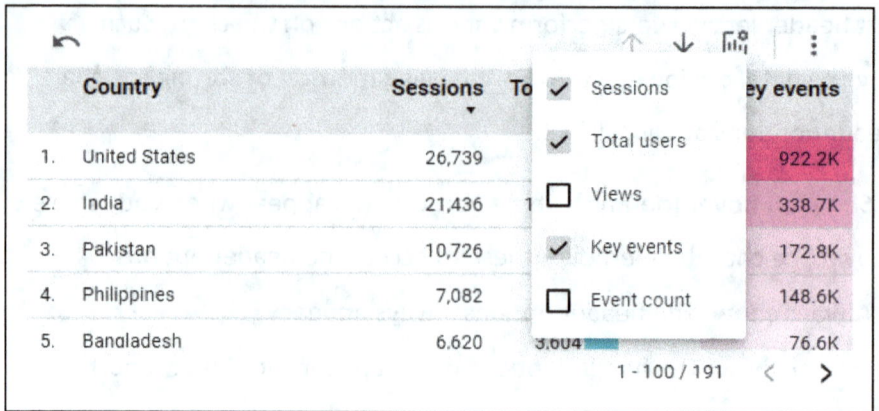

Figure 33. Table chart with optional metrics selection shown in the table header

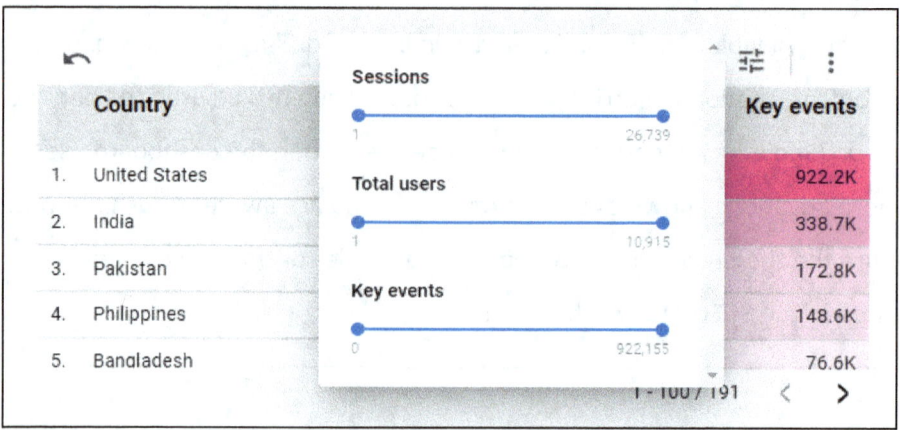

Figure 34. Table chart with metric sliders

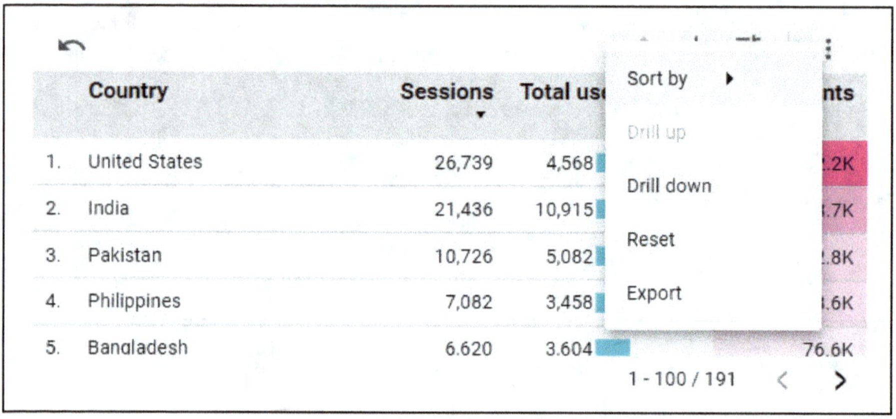

Figure 35. Table header options

Grids

- **Axis and Grid Color**: Set colors for the axis and grid lines settings to enhance readability.
- **Font Settings & Position**: Customize the font type, metric label positioning, and size for grid lines and labels.

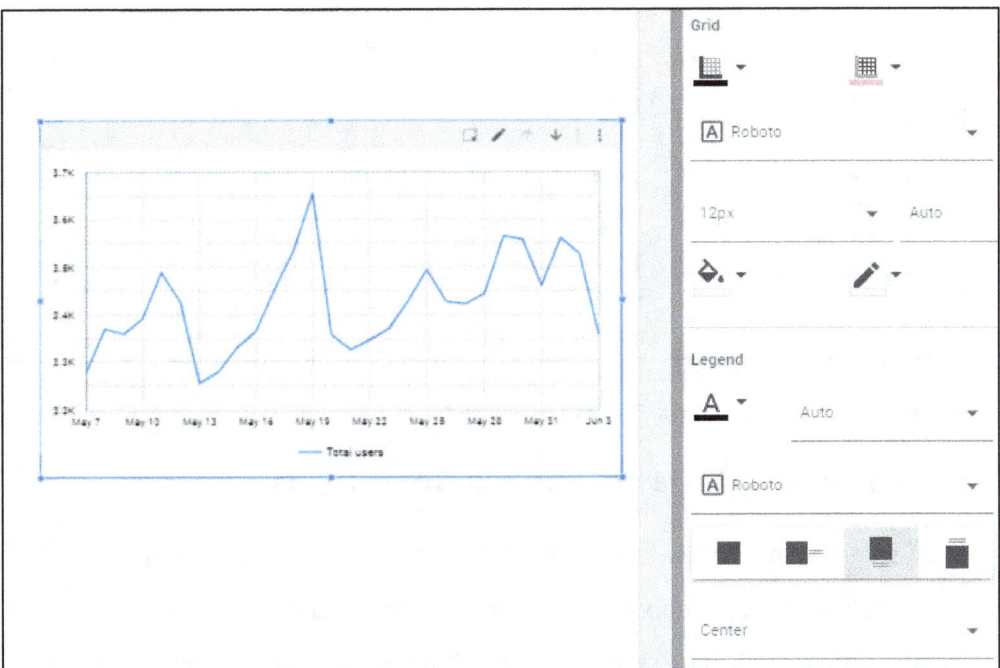

Figure 36. Styling the grid

Background and Borders

- **Background and Border Color**: Set the background and border colors of the chart.
- **Border Radius**: Add rounded borders to the chart background for a polished look.
- **Opacity**: Adjust the chart's opacity to control its transparency.
- **Border Weight and Style**: Set the thickness and style of the border lines.

- **Border Shadow**: Add a shadow to the chart's borders for a three-dimensional effect.

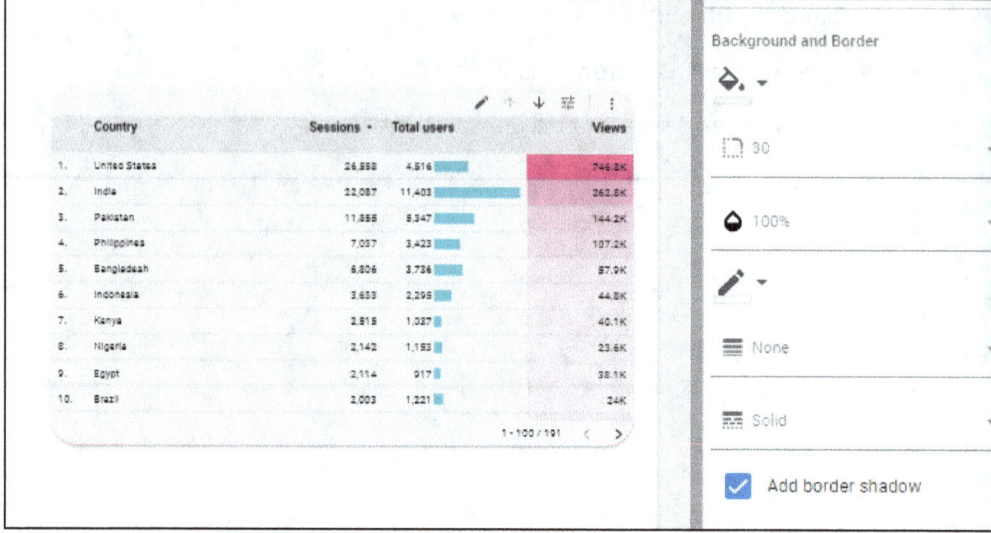

Figure 37. Setting border and background styles

Changing Main Styles of Various Chart Types

Main style settings for various chart types refer to the ability to change the general style of charts, allowing for different visual representations of your data. By styles on an individual chart component in your dashboards, you can achieve various looks and formats in your graphs and tables. Such configurations can be particularly useful for customizing the appearance of your visualizations to match your specific design requirements. Otherwise, it is recommended to set up such common configurations on a theme level as explained previously.

Common options in the style section across various charts include:

- **Setting Label Colors, Font, and Font Size**: You can customize the colors, font types, and sizes of the labels to enhance readability and align with your design aesthetics.

- **Setting Background Color**: This includes options for solid colors, gradients, and transparency levels to control the look of the chart's background.
- **Setting Border Properties**: You can adjust the border color, border radius, and border shadow to add depth and definition to your charts.

Additionally, it is always possible to reset all custom settings by clicking on "Reset to report theme" to the report's original theme settings, providing a quick way to revert to the default look and feel.

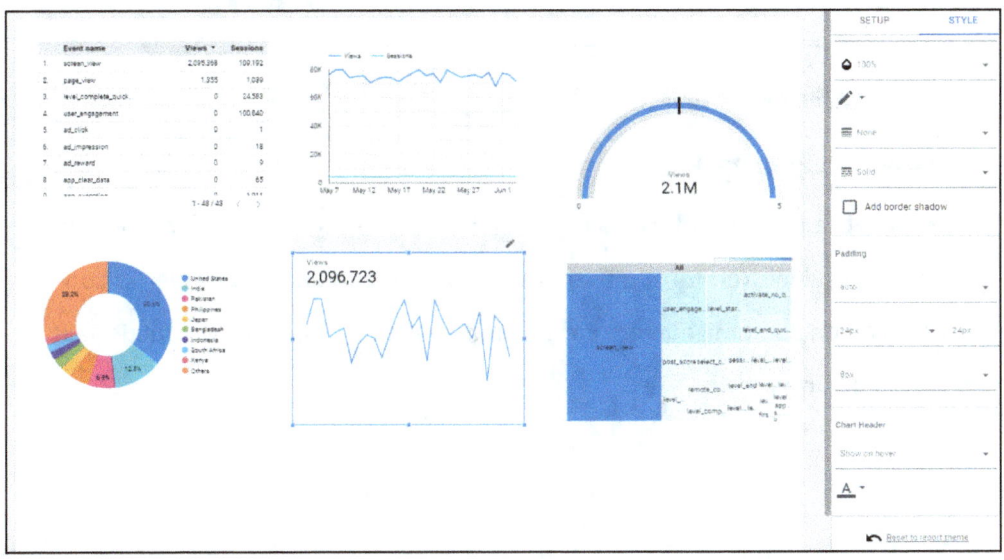

Figure 38. General chart styling

Copying and Pasting Styles Between Charts

In Looker Studio, you can easily replicate styles from one chart to another. To do this, right-click on the chart you want to copy styles from, select "Copy," then right-click on the target chart, and choose "Paste Special" > "Paste Styles only." This allows you to maintain a consistent look across your charts without manually adjusting each style setting.

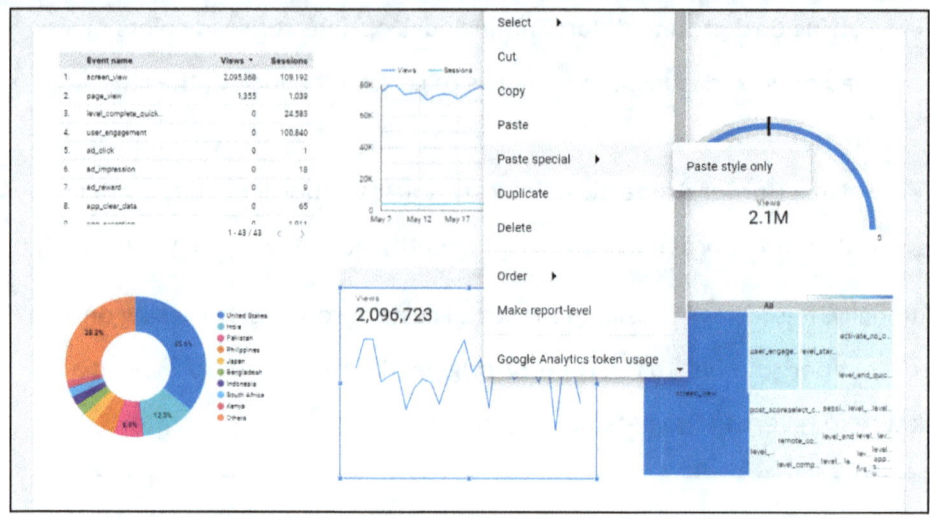

Figure 39. Pasting styles on a chart

Table Visualizations

The table is a fundamental chart type in data visualization, transforming raw data into a structured format that is easy to read and analyze. Tables in Looker Studio can be customized with various features to enhance their functionality and visual appeal.

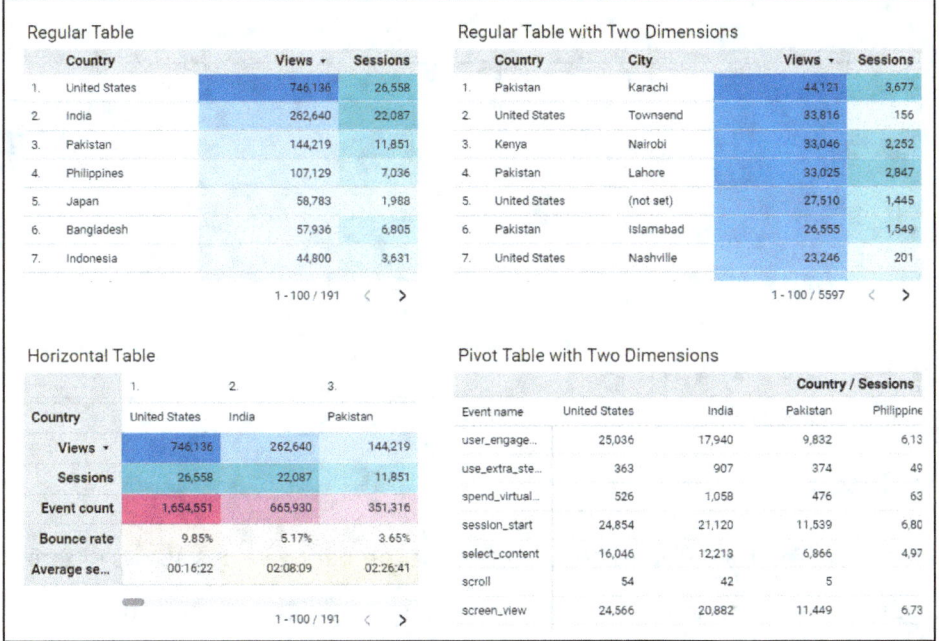

Figure 40. Different table chart variations

Variations

Table with Bars: This variation adds horizontal bars to the table cells, providing a visual representation of the data's magnitude. This is useful when comparing values within a column.

Table with Heatmap: A heatmap is a graphical representation of data where the individual values contained in a matrix are represented as colors. In the context of a table, this variation uses color gradients to highlight the magnitude of values, making it easier to identify patterns and trends.

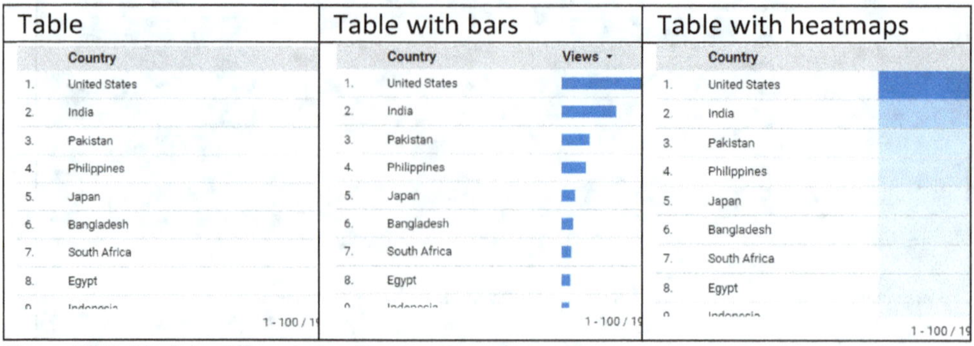

Figure 41. Table data different visualizations formats

Use Cases

Comparative Analysis: Tables are effective for comparing values across different categories or time periods. The addition of bars or a heatmap can further emphasize these comparisons, making it easier to identify outliers or trends.

Data Exploration: Tables are ideal for displaying large datasets that require sorting and filtering. The interactive nature of Looker Studio's tables allows users to explore the data in detail, facilitating data-driven decision-making.

Performance Metrics: Tables with bars can be used to display performance metrics, such as sales figures or KPIs, allowing stakeholders to quickly assess performance and identify areas for improvement.

Styling Tables in Looker Studio

Variations & Style Settings

To use multiple variations on the same table chart, you can access the style settings for individual dimensions in the Looker Studio interface and choose to show it as "Number", as a "Heatmap", or as a "Bar".

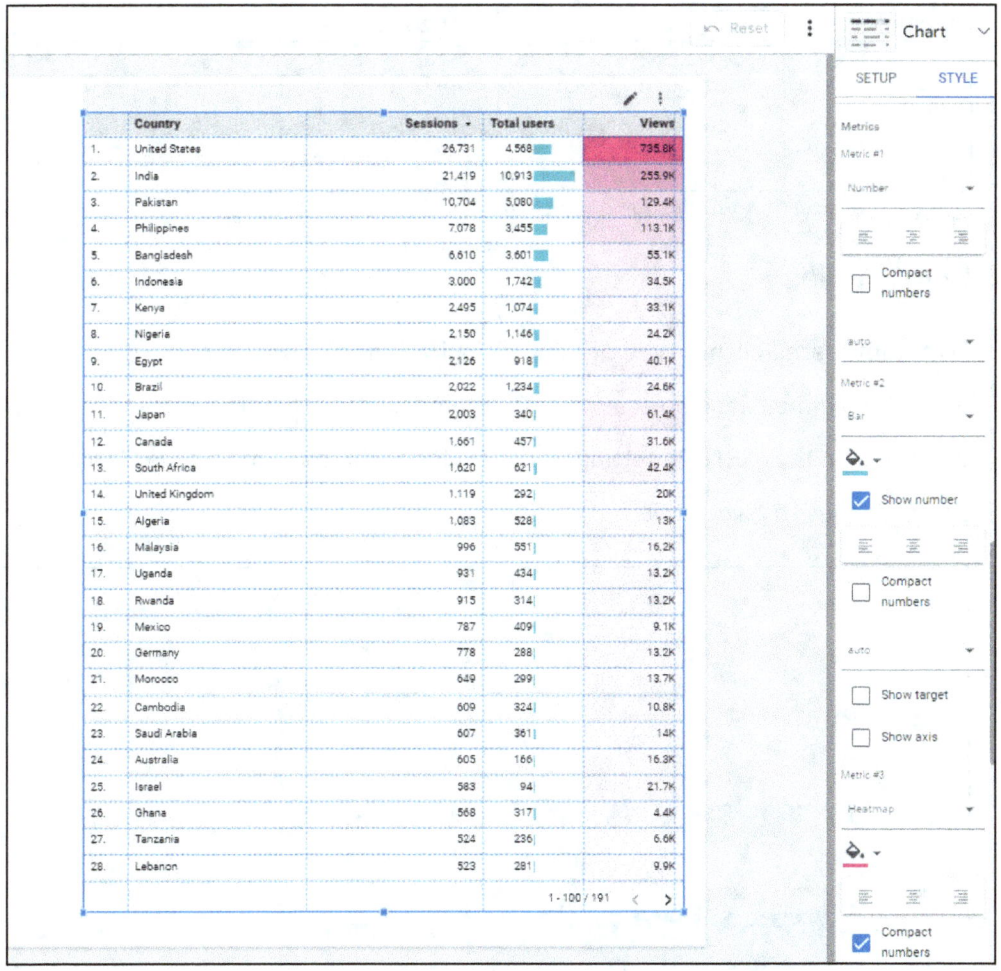

Figure 42. Long table fading heatmap data style

Table Alignment

By default, the table position is set to Vertical. To transpose the table, click the Horizontal button.

Keep in mind that horizontal positioning might not be suitable in case your dimension contains many values that you don't want to hide, as it would make it necessary to horizontally scroll through the table.

Vertical	Horizontal

Figure 43. Vertical vs. horizontal table chart alignment

Pivot Tables

Pivot tables are another type of table visualizations that would allow the usage of multiple dimensions both as rows & columns. Other than this minor difference in the "SETUP" setting, same styling techniques of all other table charts applies to pivot tables.

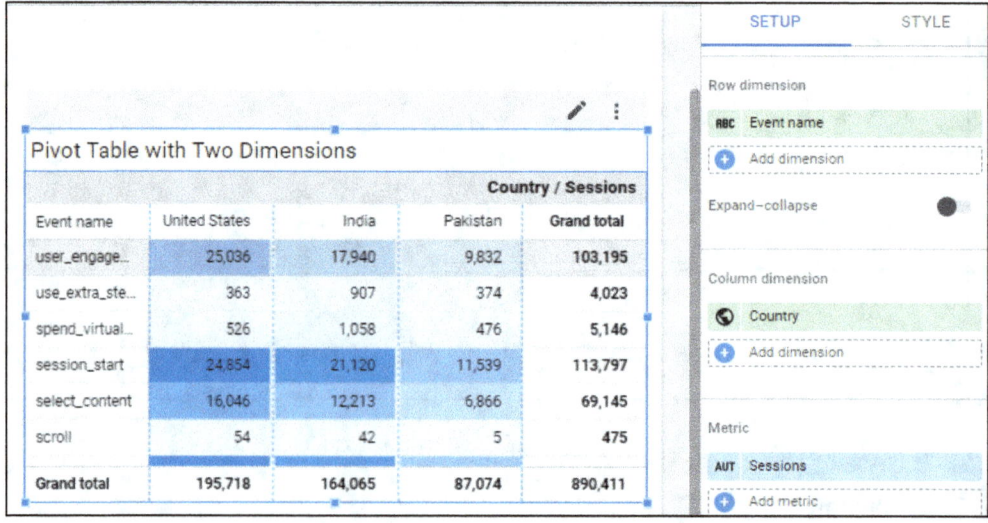

Figure 44. Pivot table with heatmap data styling

Scorecard Visualizations

Figure 45. Scorecard with previous period comparison and a trend line

Scorecards display a summary of a single metric and are commonly used to visualize key performance indicators (KPIs) or other variables that measure the relative health or performance of a business or area of activity. These simple yet powerful tools provide a quick snapshot of critical data points, making them ideal for dashboards and reports.

Examples of metrics that can be visualized using scorecards include: Total Sessions, Views, Bounce Rate, Revenue etc..

Use Cases

Scorecards are versatile and can be applied across various domains to monitor performance and track key metrics.

Here are some common use cases:

- **Business Performance Monitoring**: Scorecards can track essential business metrics such as total sales, average transaction value, customer retention rate, and other KPIs that reflect the company's overall health.
- **Website Analytics**: For web analytics, scorecards are useful for monitoring metrics like bounce rate, average session duration, total

page views, and user engagement metrics, providing insights into website performance and user behavior.
- **Ad Campaign Metrics**: In digital marketing, scorecards can summarize critical ad campaign metrics, including ad impressions, click-through rate (CTR), conversion rate, and cost-per-click (CPC), helping marketers assess the effectiveness of their campaigns.

These use cases illustrate the flexibility and utility of scorecards in providing quick, at-a-glance insights into key metrics across different areas of activity.

Variations

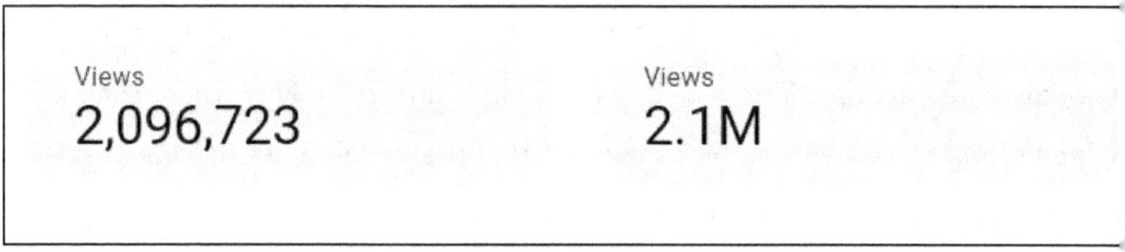

Views	Views
2,096,723	2.1M

Figure 46. Scorecard variations: full number (basic scorecard) vs. a compact number

- **Basic Scorecard**: This type of scorecard displays the number and the metric name, offering a straightforward view of the selected data.
- **Compact Scorecard**: This variation is designed for space efficiency, displaying numbers in a compact format. For instance, instead of showing 354,700 views, a compact scorecard would display 354.7K, making it easier to fit multiple scorecards on a single dashboard without sacrificing readability.

Styling Scorecards in Looker Studio

Primary Metric Styling

The primary metric is the core data point displayed on a scorecard. Here are the key styling options available for the primary metric:

Compact Numbers

Rounds numbers and displays unit indicators. For example, 553,939 becomes 553.9K, making large numbers easier to read and fit within the scorecard.

Decimal Precision

Sets the number of decimal places for the metric values, providing control over the display precision of your data.

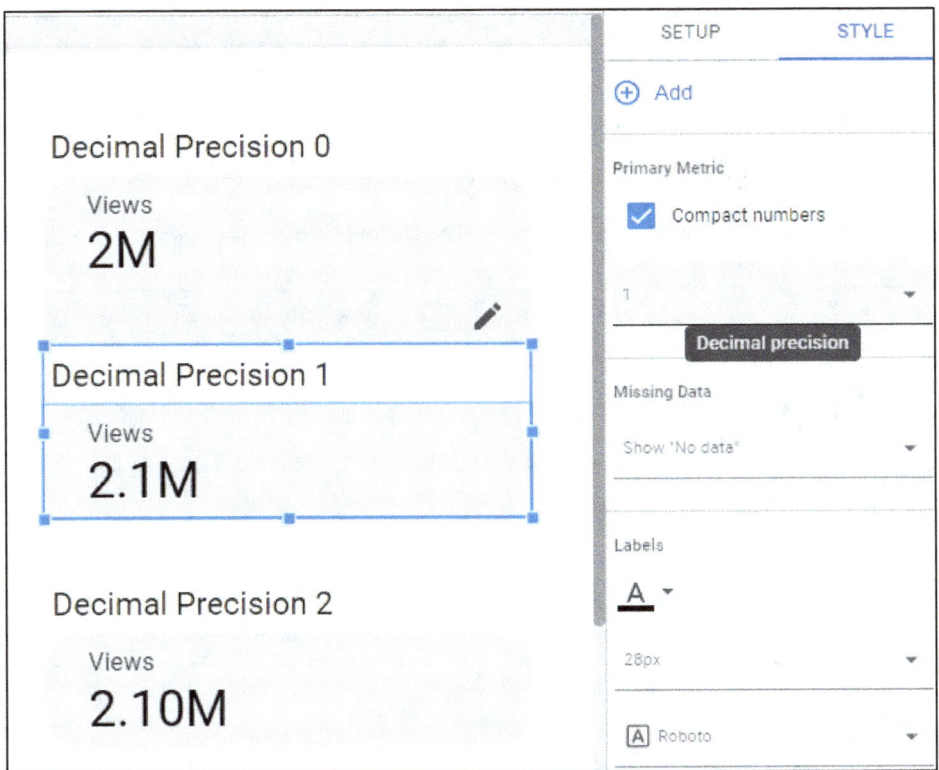

Figure 47. Decimal precision adjustment for a compact scorecard

Comparison Metrics

Scorecards can include comparison metrics to provide context and show trends over time. Here are the key styling options for comparison metrics:

Change Colors: Sets the font colors for positively and negatively trending data. Use colors like green to indicate positive performance (upward trend) and red to highlight negative performance (downward trend).

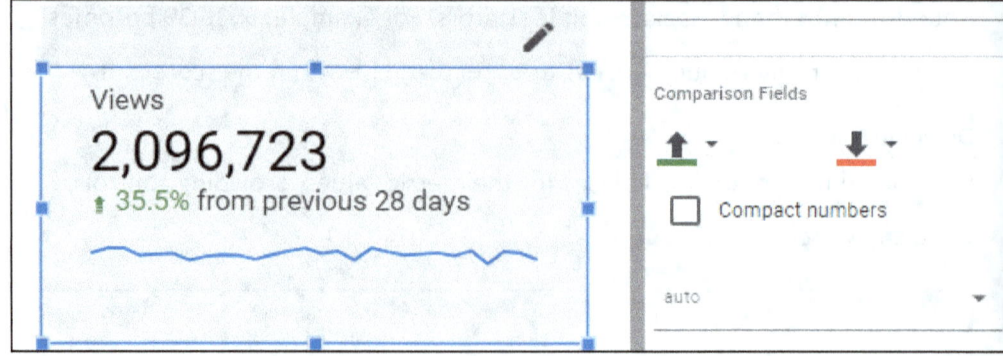

Figure 48. Previous period comparison as a percentage

Show Absolute Change: Toggles between displaying the percentage change and the absolute numeric difference, allowing for different perspectives on the data.

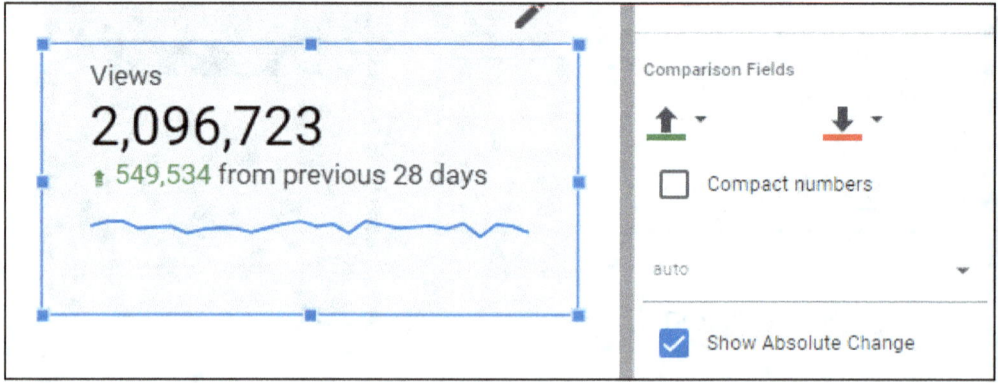

Figure 49. Previous period comparison as an absolute number

Compact Numbers: Rounds numbers and displays unit indicators for comparison metrics as well, maintaining consistency with the primary metric display.

Decimal Precision: Sets the number of decimal places for the comparison values.

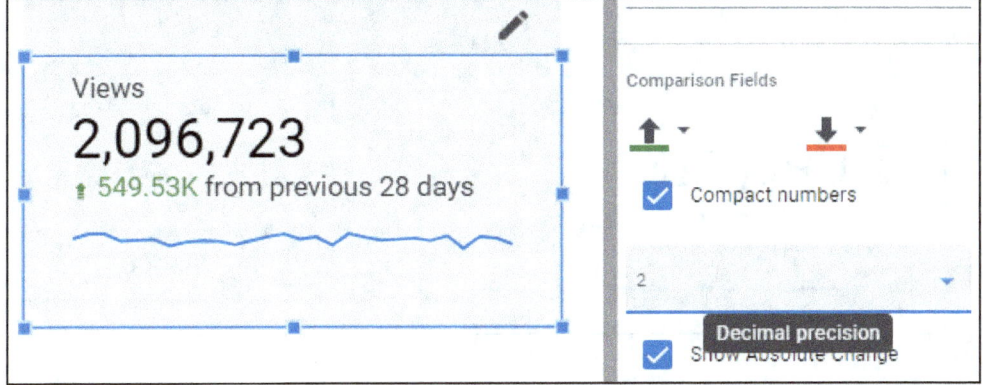

Figure 50. Previous period comparison as an absolute compact number

Hide Comparison Label: Hides the label that shows the comparison period, providing a cleaner look if the label is not needed.

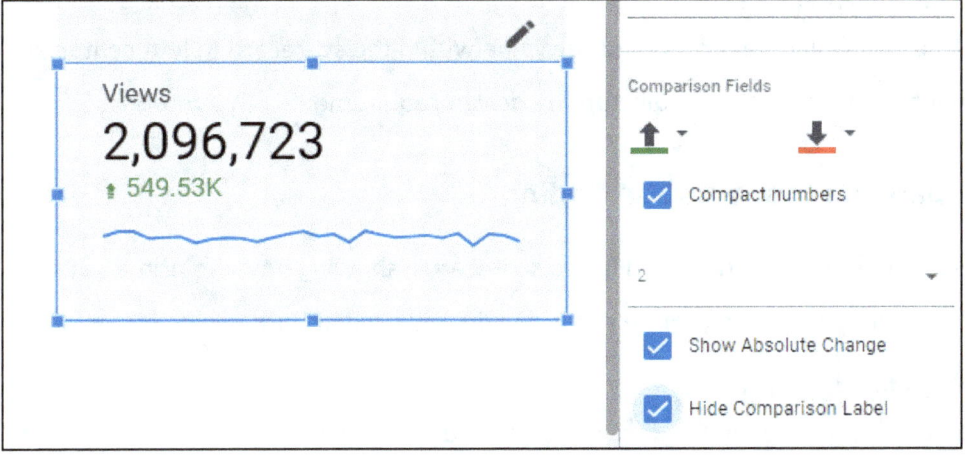

Figure 51. Previous period comparison with a hidden label

Comparison Label: Customize the comparison label to provide context, such as "Q4 new users" or "Last month vs. this month," enhancing the clarity of the data comparison.

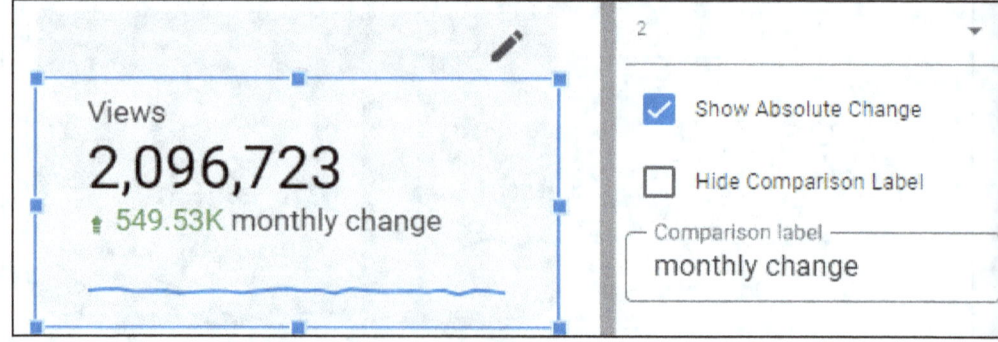

Figure 52. Previous period comparison with a custom label

Font Size, Color, and Style

Customize the font size, color, and style (bold, italic, underline) to ensure the primary metric is easily readable and visually appealing.

Padding & Alignment

Adjust the alignment of the metric value within the scorecard to left, center, or right, up, or down depending on the design requirements of your report.

Sparkline Visualization Styling

Sparklines add a visual trendline to scorecards, showing how the primary metric has changed over time. Here's how to add and style a sparkline:

Steps to Add a Sparkline

Select the Scorecard: Click on the scorecard to which you want to add a sparkline.

Open Setup Tab: In the Properties panel on the right, go to the Setup tab.

Add Dimension: In the Sparkline section, click on the "Add dimension" option.

Select Date Dimension: Choose the desired date dimension from the drop-down menu to use as the basis for the sparkline.

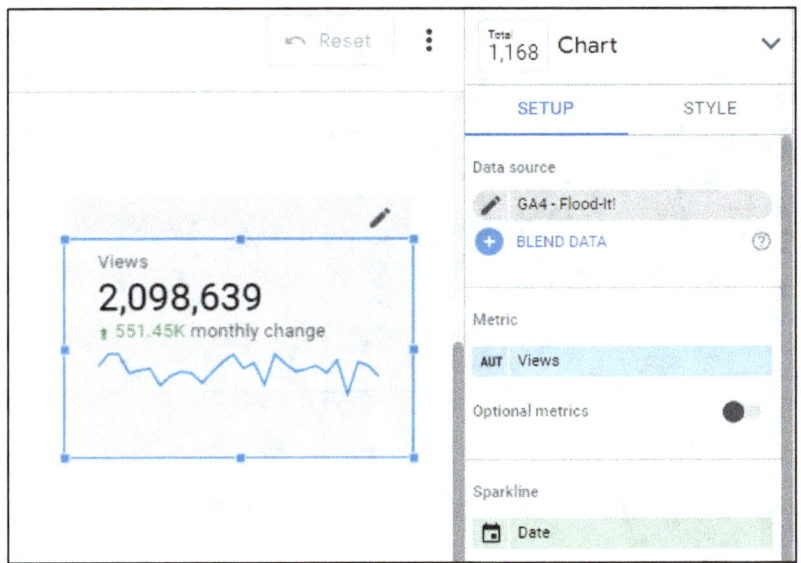

Figure 53. Scorecard with "Date" as a sparkline dimension

Sparkline Styling Options

- **Sparkline Color**: Change the color of the sparkline to match your report's theme or to make it stand out.

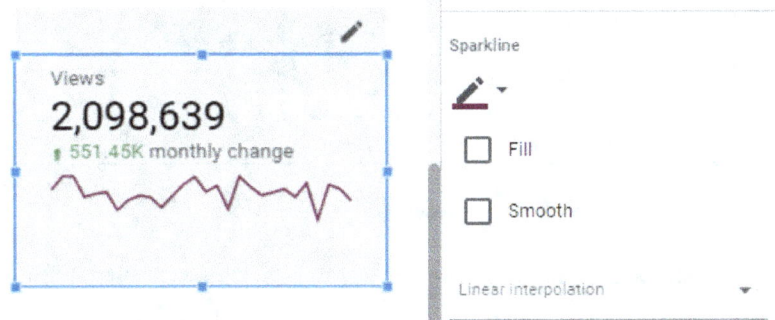

Figure 54. A scorecard with modified sparkline color

- **Fill**: Fill the area under the sparkline with a lighter shade of the sparkline color, enhancing visual impact.

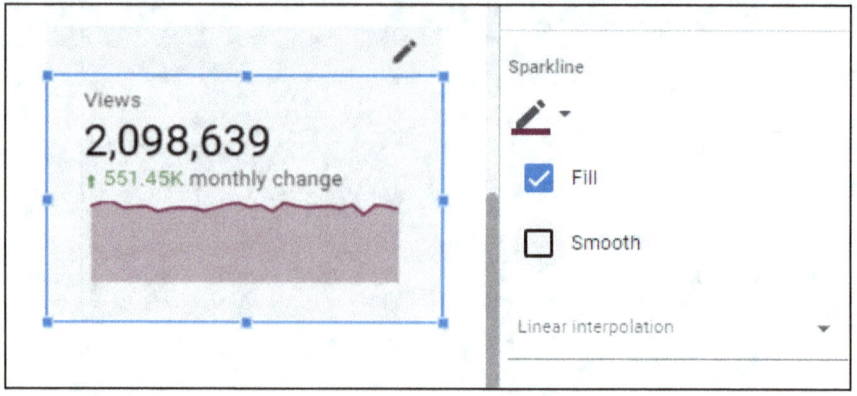

Figure 55. A scorecard with a sparkline filled area

- **Smooth**: Display series lines as curves instead of straight lines, providing a smoother appearance.

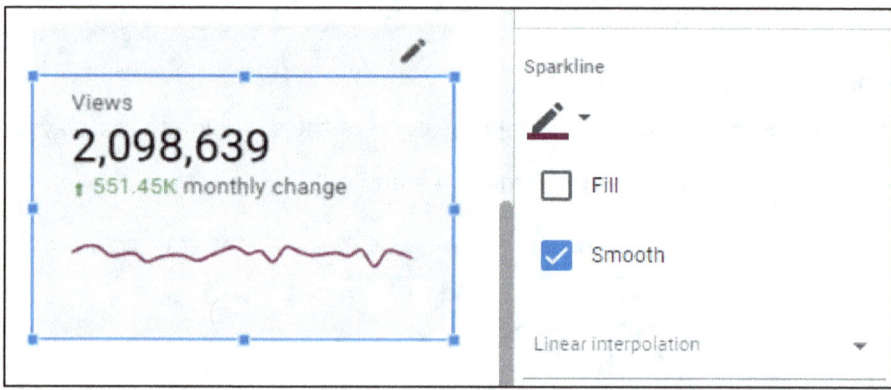

Figure 56. A scorecard with a smooth sparkline

- Missing Data Handling: Set how the sparkline will display missing data with options like Line to Zero (drop to zero), Line Breaks (breaks in data), or Linear Interpolation (connects data points across missing data).
- Progress Visual: The "Show as progress" setting under the "SETUP" tab allows to visualize the progress of your primary metric toward a target value. This setting is part of the comparison settings, but using this type of visualization would eliminate the possibility of having a sparkline that would be substituted with the progress visualization.

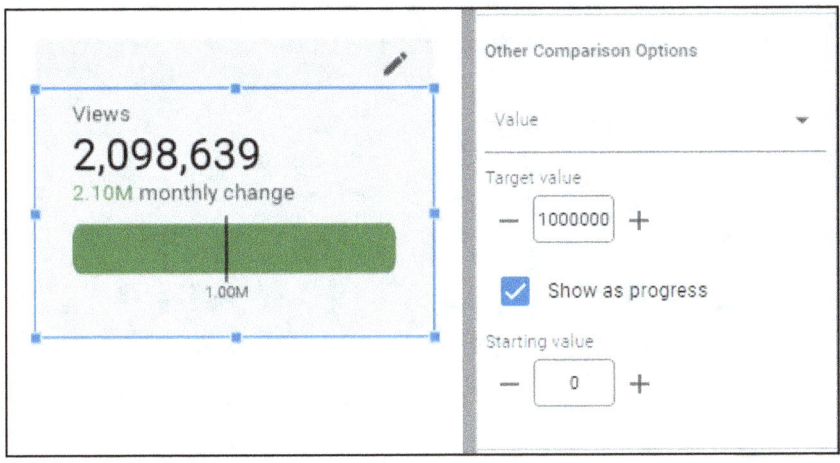

Figure 57. A scorecard with a progress visual indicator

Time Series Visualizations

A time series chart in Looker Studio displays a trend of how data changes over a period of time. It is an essential tool for visualizing trends, patterns, and fluctuations within your data. The X-axis represents always a time dimension, while the Y-axis shows the measurement scale of the data being tracked. Time series charts are versatile and can accommodate up to five different metrics, each represented as a line or bar. This allows for a comprehensive analysis of how various data points evolve simultaneously. Whether you are monitoring website traffic, financial performance, or user engagement, time series charts provide a clear and intuitive way to track changes and make data-driven decisions. It is important not to confuse time series charts with other trendline charts that we will be covering next.

Figure 58. Time series chart with a previous period comparison

Use Cases

Performance Trend Analysis
Performance Trend Analysis involves tracking and analyzing performance trends over time to identify growth, stagnation, or decline in key metrics.

Seasonality and Pattern Identification
Seasonality and Pattern Identification focuses on recognizing recurring patterns or seasonal trends in data, helping to understand the impact of seasonal variations on performance.

Monitoring and Forecasting
Monitoring and Forecasting entails continuous monitoring of metrics and using historical data to make informed predictions about future performance.

Anomaly Detection

Anomaly Detection is about identifying outliers or unusual patterns in data that deviate from expected behavior, which could indicate errors, fraud, or significant changes in performance.

Impact Analysis

Impact Analysis involves assessing the effects of specific events, actions, or factors on performance metrics to understand causality and make informed decisions.

Comparative Analysis

Comparative Analysis entails comparing the performance of different segments, time periods, or entities to identify trends, patterns, and areas for improvement.

Time Series Variations

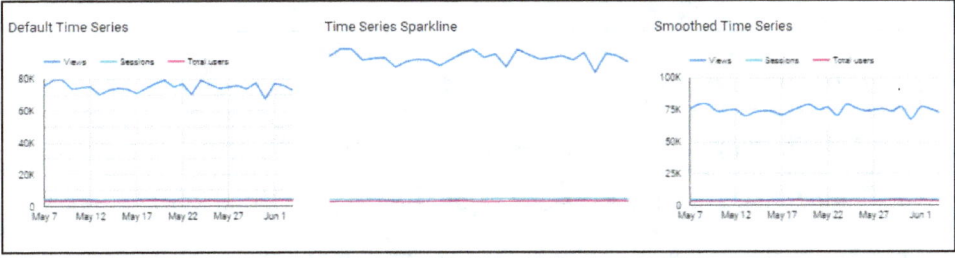

Figure 59. Time series variations examples

- **Sparkline Chart:** A compact, inline version of the time series chart, often used to provide a quick overview of trends within a constrained space.
- **Smoothed Time Series Chart:** A variation of the time series chart where the data points are connected with a smoothed line, reducing noise and highlighting overall trends.

Styling Time Series Charts in Looker Studio

Series

Series refer to the different metrics used in the chart. The series will be numbered from 1 to 5. It is possible to style them as follows:

- **Line or Bars**: Choose to display data points as lines or bars. Lines are useful for trends, while bars can show comparisons.

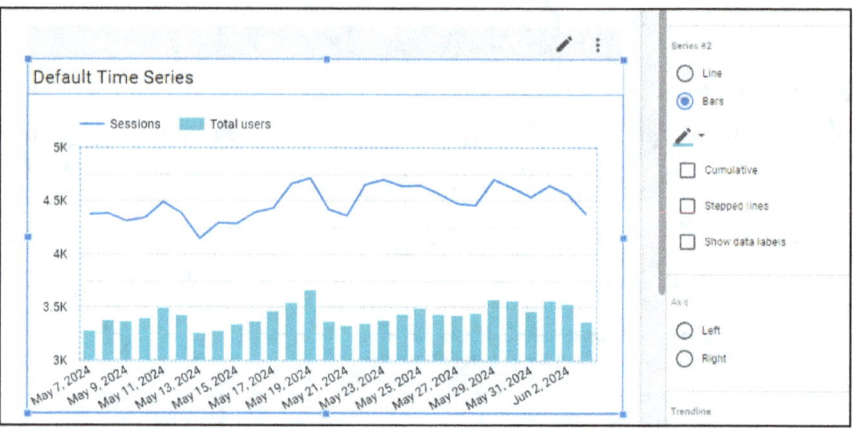

Figure 60. Time series chart with one of the series showing as a bar

- **Line Weight**: Set the thickness of the line series.
- **Line Style**: Customize the appearance of the line (solid, dashed, etc.).
- **Series Color**: Set the color for the series line or bar.
- **Cumulative**: Sum data over time, showing an accumulating total.
- **Show Points**: Display individual data points on a line series. This helps highlight specific values.

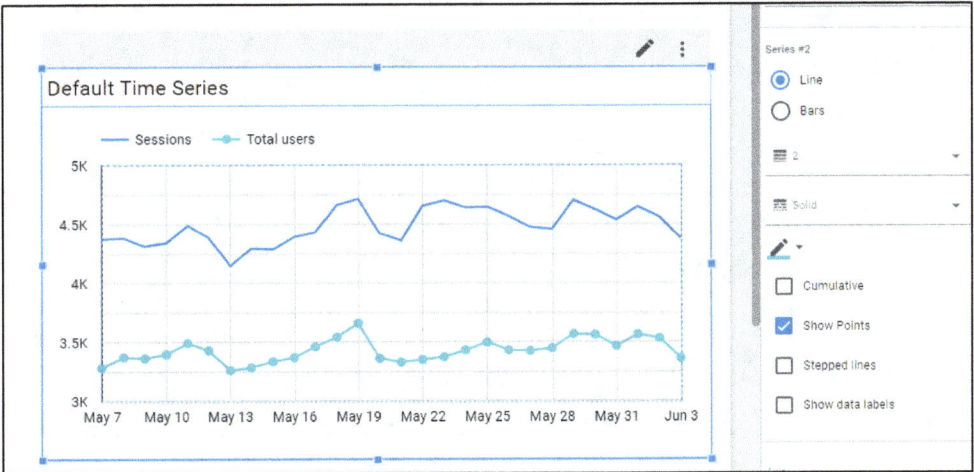

Figure 61. Plotted data points on one of the series

- **Show Data Labels**: Display individual values for the data points in the series.

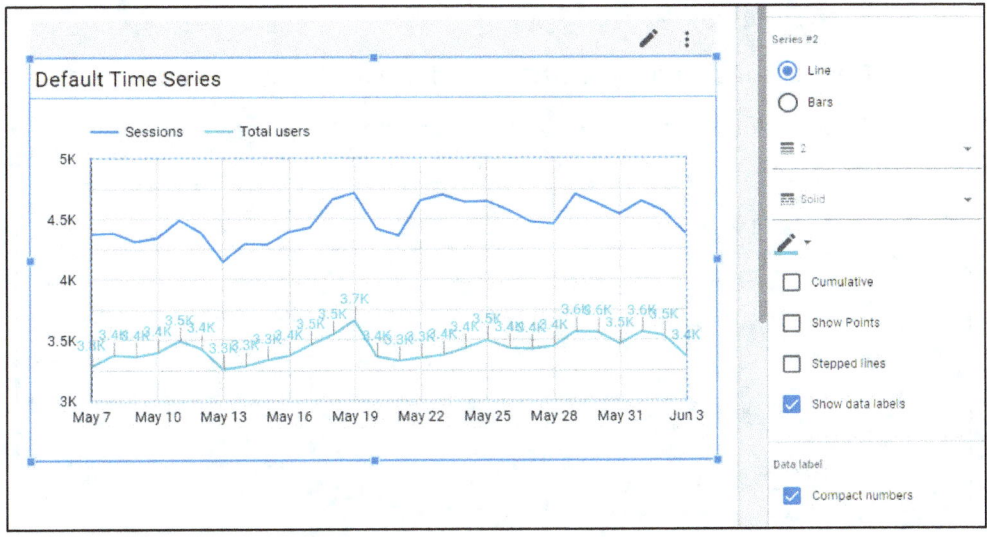

Figure 62. Showing captions on one of the series

- **Stepped Lines**: Show a series of steps between data points instead of a smooth line, useful for visualizing step changes.

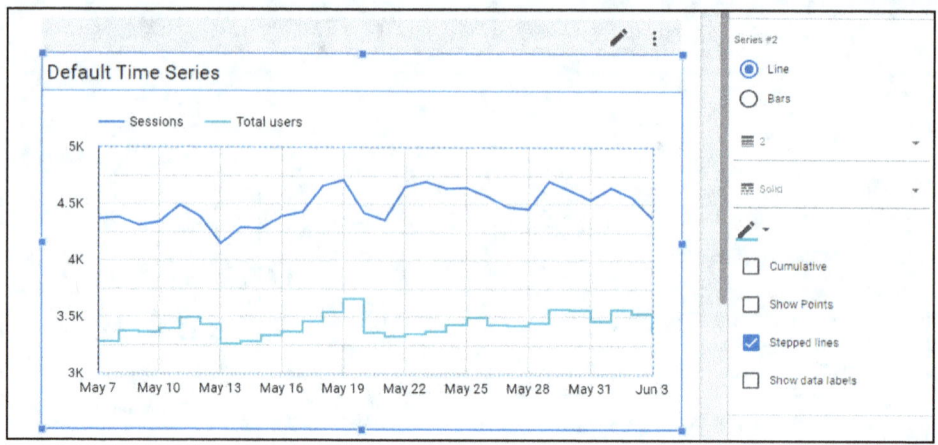

Figure 63. One of the series shown as a stepped line

- **Compact Numbers**: Rounds numbers and displays the unit indicator (e.g., 553,939 becomes 553.9K).
- **Decimal Precision**: Set the number of decimal places to display for metric values.
- **Trendline**: Add a trendline to show the overall direction of the data. Types include linear, polynomial, exponential, and moving average.

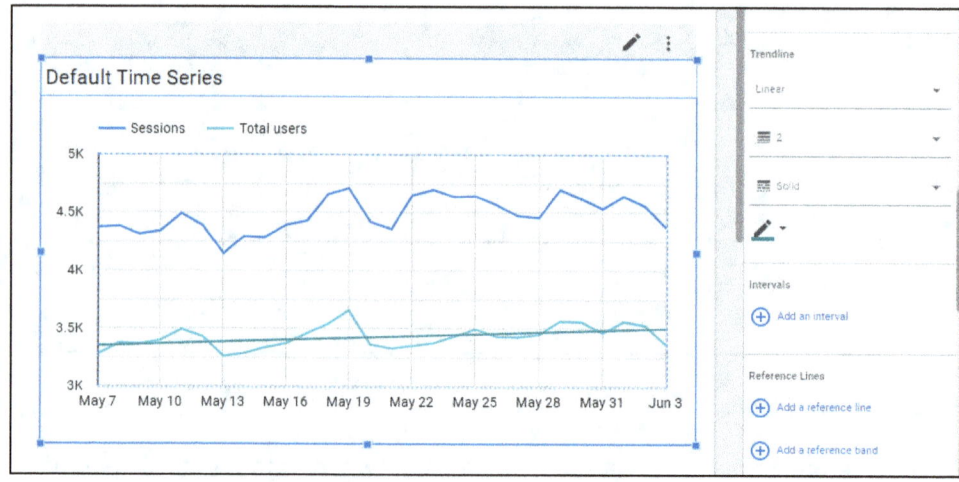

Figure 64. Adding a trend line to one of the series

- **Intervals**: Visualize data intervals by adding interval areas to your time series chart.

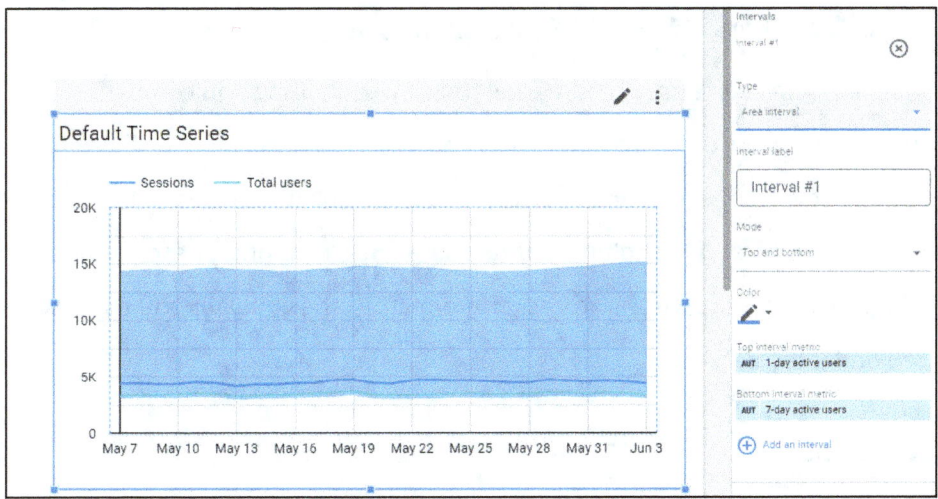

Figure 65. Adding an interval area to the chart

- **Reference lines**: Add lines or bands to highlight specific values or ranges in your chart.

Figure 66. Adding a reference line to the chart

Bar & Column Charts Visualizations

Bar and column charts are fundamental tools for visualizing and comparing different categories of information. They represent data using bars, where the length (or height) of each bar correlates with the value it represents. Bar charts use horizontal bars, while column charts use vertical columns. These charts are ideal for making comparisons across different categories, making trends easier to see and interpret.

Use Cases

Bar and column charts are versatile and can be used in various scenarios

Single Dimension with Multiple Metrics
This method allows you to analyze a single category using up to 20 metrics. For instance, you can display sales data over several years to see growth trends across different metrics like revenue, profit, and units sold.

Two or More Dimensions with a Single Metric
This method applies a breakdown dimension to the primary dimension, measuring the breakdown with a single metric. An example would be showing annual sales data broken down by region or sales associate to see which areas or individuals are performing best.

Stacked Charts
Use stacked bar or column charts to show part-to-whole relationships. This is useful for visualizing the contribution of different components to a whole, such as the market share of different brands within a sector.

Variations

Looker Studio offers four variations of the standard bar and column charts:

Figure 67. Different variations of bar and column charts

Bar Charts

- **Stacked Bar Chart**: Displays breakdown dimensions stacked horizontally.
- **100% Stacked Bar Chart**: Each series in the chart has the same overall length, showing the part-to-whole relationships.

Column Charts

- **Stacked Column Chart**: Breakdown dimensions are stacked vertically.
- **100% Stacked Column Chart**: Each series in the chart has the same overall height, ideal for showing part-to-whole relationships.

Styling of Bar & Colum Charts in Looker Studio

Styling of this type of charts is straightforward and in line with most of the common styling settings. Additional style settings involve the below details:

Bar/Column Orientation

Vertical: For column charts.

Horizontal: For bar charts.

Bars/Column

- **Number of Series**: Specify how many data series are shown. If fewer than the data's series, only the top N series will be shown.
- **Stacked Bars/Columns**: Enable to display stacked bars or columns. Otherwise, they will be grouped.
- **100% Stacking**: Shows the contribution of each data series to 100% of the total value.
- **Show Total Card**: Shows the total value of the metrics for a selected stacked bar or column.

Data Labels

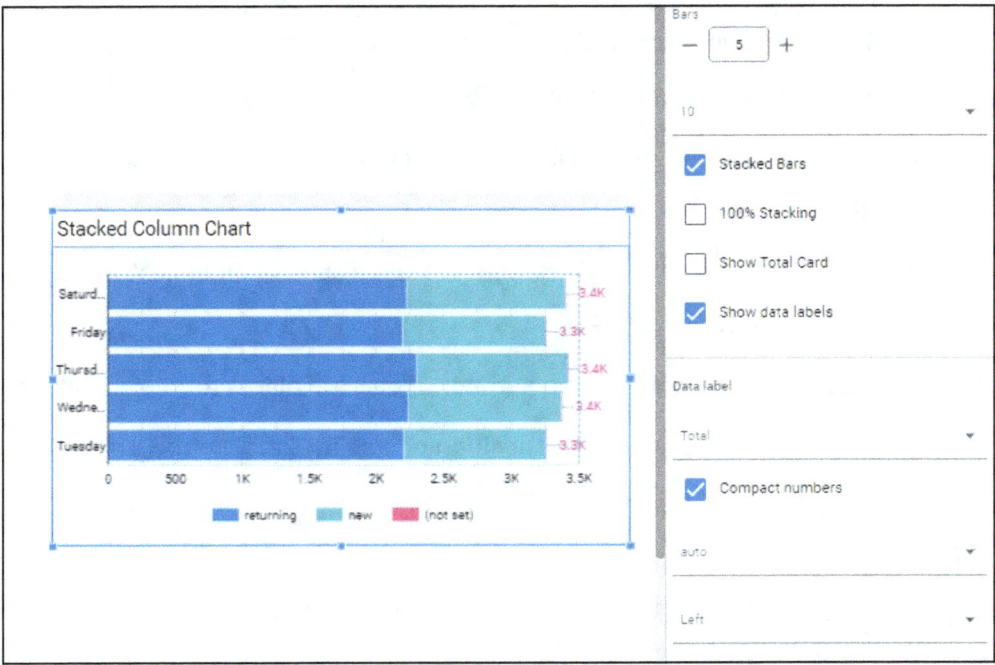

Figure 68. Adding data labels to a column chart

- **Show Data Labels**: Display the value for each series.
- **Bar Label Type**: For stacked charts, choose between metric value, stacked value, or total stack value.
- **Show Data Label As**: Numbers or percentages (available for 100% stacked charts).
- **Compact Numbers**: Rounds numbers and displays unit indicators (e.g., 553,939 becomes 553.9K).
- **Decimal Precision**: Sets the number of decimal places for metric values.
- **Bar Label Position**: Sets the position of labels relative to the bar or column.

Color by
- **Single Color**: Displays data series in shades of a single color.
- **Series Order**: Colors the data according to its position.

Dimension Values: Ensures consistent color use for each dimension value.

Bar Border Color

Customize the outline color for the bars or columns.

Reference Lines

Add reference lines or bands to highlight specific values or ranges.

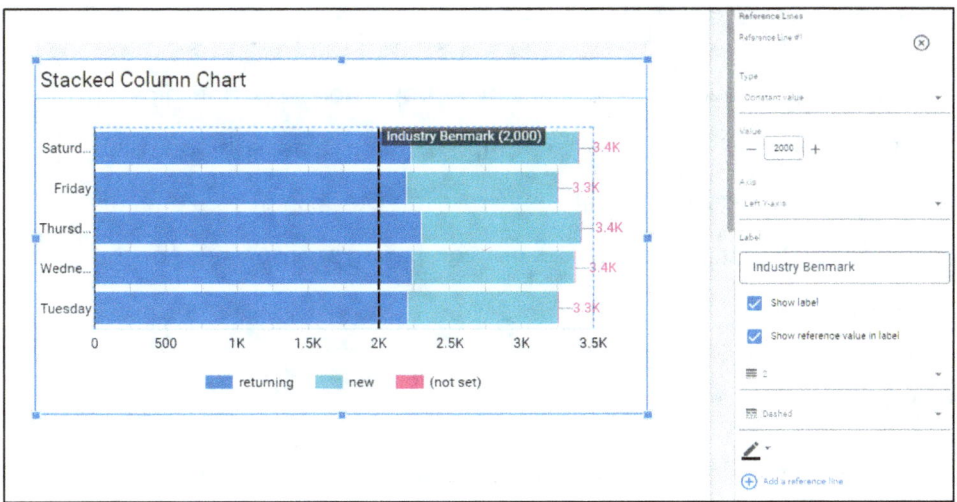

Figure 69. Adding a reference line indicator to a column chart

Pie Visualizations

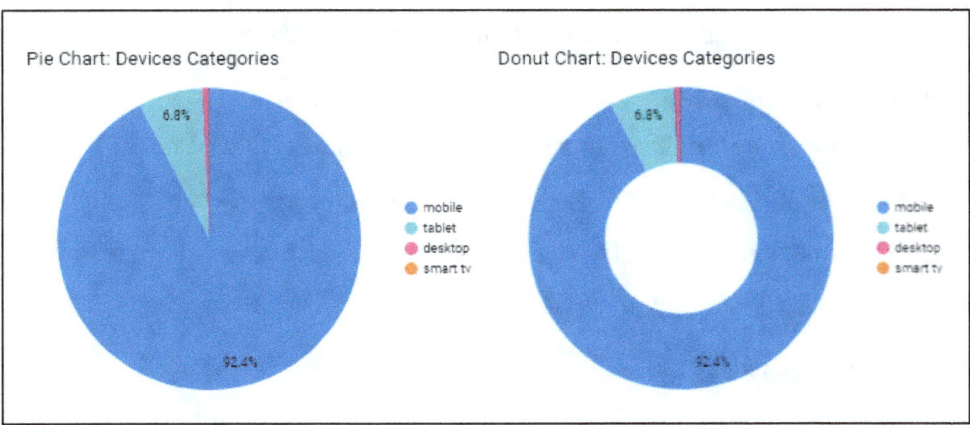

Figure 70. Pie visualization variations: Full pie vs. donut chart

Pie charts are widely used in data visualization to represent the composition or distribution of a dataset. They are circular in shape, resembling a pie cut into slices, where each slice represents a proportionate part of the whole. The size of each slice is determined by the value it represents relative to the total value of the dataset, making it easy to compare the relative sizes of different categories at a glance.

Pie charts are effective in conveying simple proportional relationships and are particularly useful when you want to emphasize the relative importance of individual categories within a dataset. However, they can be less effective than other chart types, such as bar charts, for comparing precise values or showing trends over time.

Use Cases

Pie charts shine on your dashboards particularly for the following use cases:

Distribution Analysis

Pie charts are ideal for showing the distribution of a single categorical variable. For example, they can be used to visualize the market share of different products or the distribution of budget allocations across departments.

Part-to-Whole Comparison

Pie charts are great for illustrating how parts contribute to a whole. They can effectively show what percentage or proportion each category contributes to the total, making them useful for visualizing survey responses, expenditure breakdowns, or demographic distributions.

Focus on Relative Sizes

Pie charts can highlight the largest or smallest slice to draw attention to a specific data point. This can be useful when you want to emphasize a particularly significant category or outlier in your data.

Percentage Representation

Pie charts can display data as percentages of a whole, providing a quick and intuitive way to understand the relative importance of different categories. This makes them valuable for presentations or reports where you want to communicate proportions clearly.

Comparison of Few Categories

Pie charts are most effective when used to compare a small number of categories (typically less than six). Beyond this, the chart can become cluttered and difficult to interpret, and other chart types like bar charts may be more suitable.

Variations

Donut Chart

A donut chart is a variation of the pie chart that includes a hole in the center. This variation allows for the display of additional information in the center of the chart, such as data labels, visuals, text or any other annotations. Donut charts can be visually appealing and provide a different way to present part-to-whole relationships while maintaining the advantages of a pie chart.

Styling Pie & Donut Charts in Looker Studio

Styling a pie chart in Google Looker Studio is relatively simple, as most of the styling settings are common styles mentioned earlier in this book. The most relevant styling options for pie charts include:

Coloring the Chart Segments
- By a single-color variant.
- By a certain order to be configured.
- By dimension values (as set on the master theme).

Thickness of the Donut Ring

Adjusting the thickness of the donut ring in the case of a donut chart.

These options allow you to customize the visual appeal and clarity of your pie chart while maintaining consistency with your overall design aesthetics.

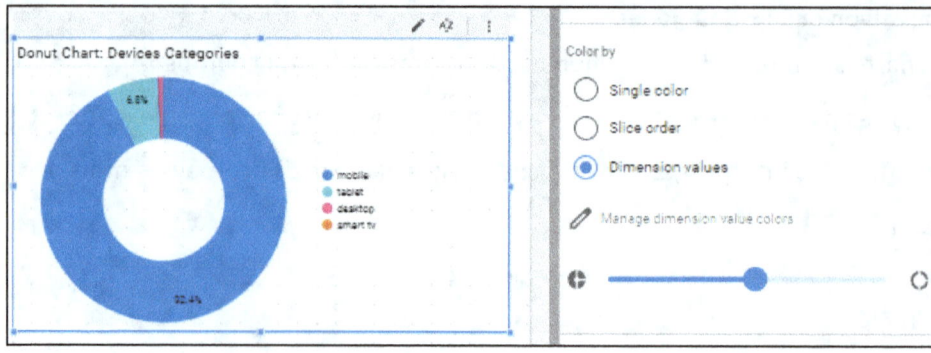

Figure 71. Adjusting the donut ring

Geo Charts Maps Visualizations

Geo Charts Maps visualizations in Looker Studio enable the display of geographic data in a highly interactive and engaging manner. These visualizations are particularly effective for projects involving location-based analytics and geographic data exploration. The geographical coordinates must be already provided your one of the dimensions in your data set according to Google Maps Geocoding API.

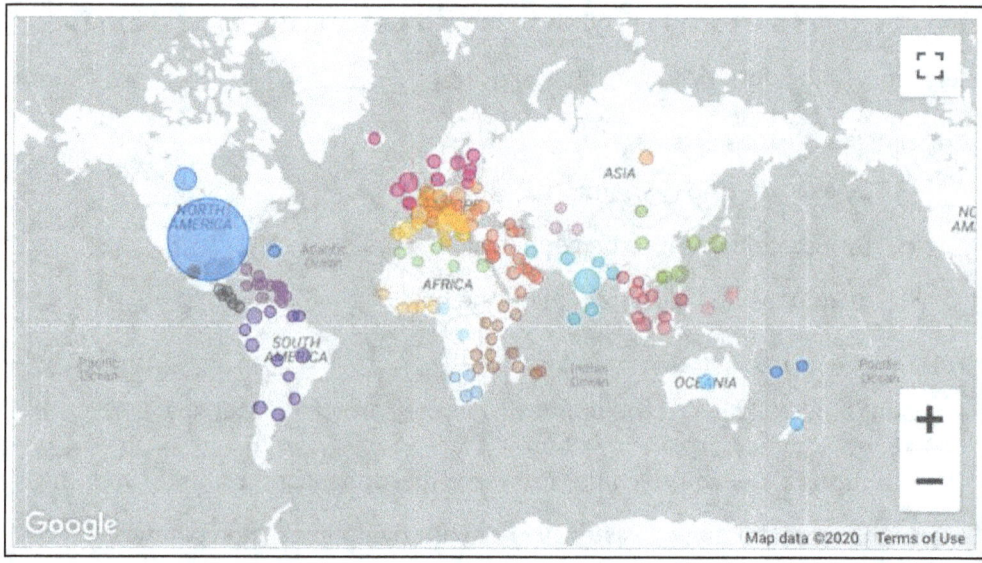

Figure 72. Map visualization with bubbles

If you simply intend to use data provided by Google Analytics, you can use any of the existing dimensions such as "Country" or "City".

Ideal for geographic data analysis, such as tracking sales by region, visualizing distribution networks, or mapping demographic distributions across different geographic areas. This visualization helps in making spatial patterns and relationships between locations clear and intuitive.

Variations and Styling Focus

Variations in Google Maps visualizations offer diverse ways to display and analyze geographic data within Looker Studio. Each variation is designed to highlight different aspects of data through unique visual techniques, accommodating a broad range of analytical needs and enhancing the interpretability of spatial information. From heat maps that illustrate data density to line maps that trace routes, these variations provide valuable insights tailored to specific use cases, making geographic data more accessible and actionable for users. You can customize markers, heat maps, and area overlays to represent different data densities or categories effectively. The color scales and icons can be adjusted to match the data's context and significance.

- **Bubble Map**: Marks data points with bubbles, size-coded according to data magnitude.

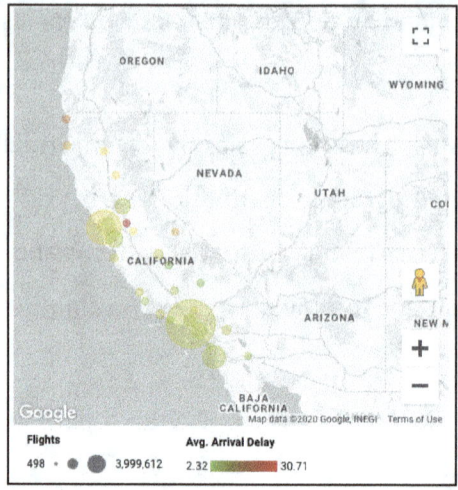

Figure 73. Map with bubbles

- **Filled Map**: Colors regions based on data values, creating a visual density map.

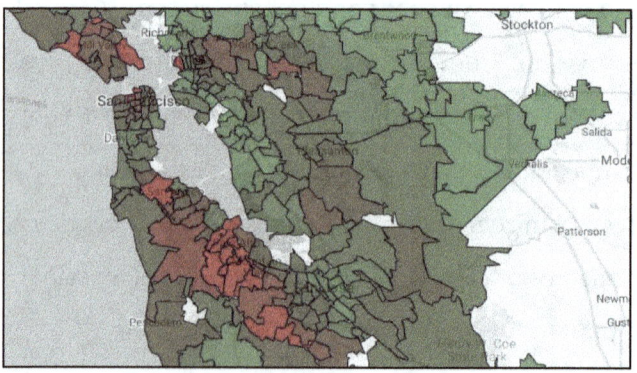

Figure 74. Filled map

- **Heat Map**: Indicates data intensity through color gradients.

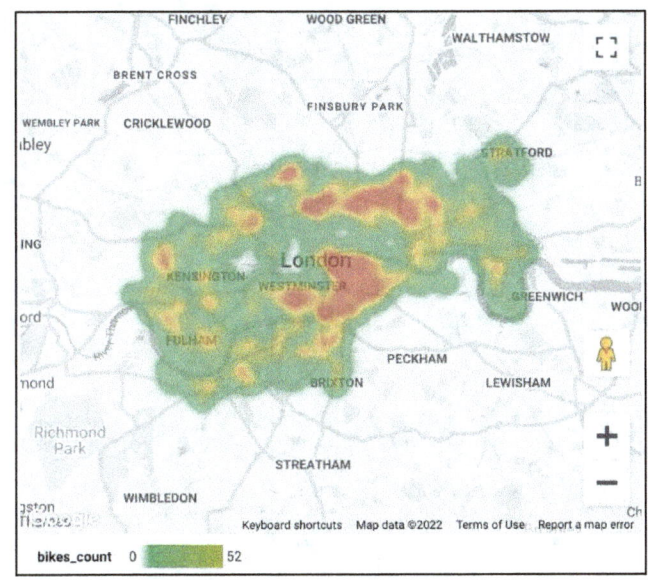

Figure 75. Heat map

- **Line Map**: Shows routes or connections between points.

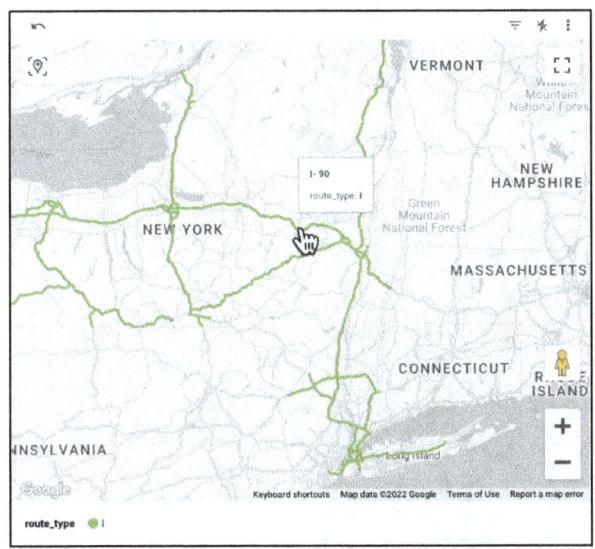

Figure 76. Lines map

- **Connection Map**: Displays lines between related geographical points, illustrating relationships or movements.

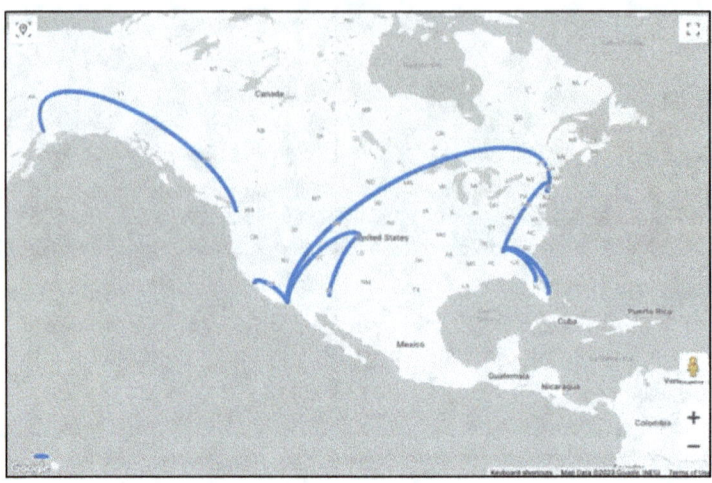

Figure 77. Connection map

- **Combo Map**: Combines any of the above features to provide multi-layered data representation.

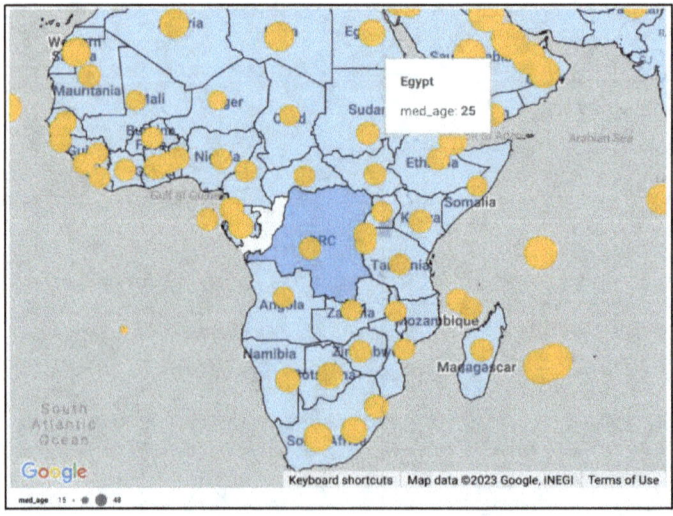

Figure 78. Combo Map

- **Geo Chart**: Simplifies geographic data visualization without the detailed geographical features of a full map.

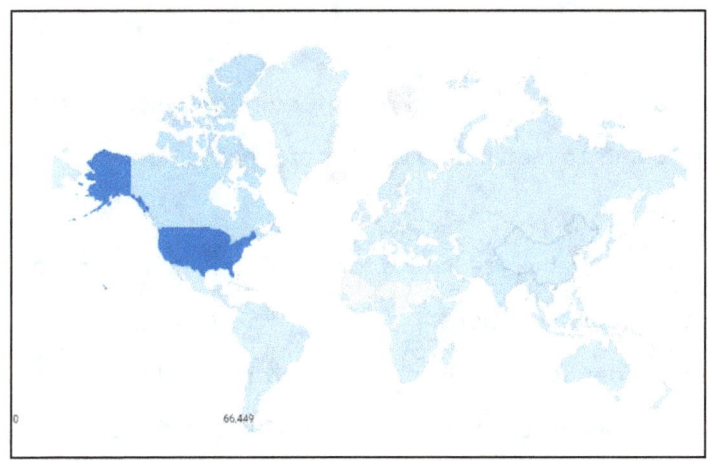

Figure 79. Geo chart (filled map)

In most of the cases, variations can be changed from the Style tab. Otherwise you would need to choose the variation type from the main charts' menu.

Map Controls

- **Navigation Controls**: Allow users to pan and zoom, enhancing interactive exploration.
- **Zoom Control**: Enables quick adjustment of the map scale.
- **Street View Control**: Allows switching to street view for on-ground visualization.
- **Fullscreen Control**: Lets users expand the map to full screen for detailed analysis.
- **Map Type Control**: Provides options to switch between map types (e.g., road map, satellite).
- **Scale Control**: Displays a scale bar to understand distances within the map.

Styling Focus

- **Color Controls**: Customize the color schemes for different elements like regions, lines, or points to match data themes or organizational branding.
- **Legend Display**: Configurable size legend for bubble and heat maps to quantify visual data representations.
- **Background and Border** Styling: Adjust the background and borders of the map to integrate seamlessly with the overall dashboard design.

Area Charts

Area charts are a fundamental component in time-series data visualization, effectively showing how values sum up over time and providing a clear visual distinction between quantitative measures. Looker Studio offers several variations of area charts to address different analytical needs, each with specific features that can enhance the storytelling aspect of your data.

Variations of Area Charts

Regular Area Charts

Figure 80. Area chart

These charts display quantitative data graphically over time, filled from the line to the axis, which emphasizes the magnitude of changes.

Use Case: Ideal for visualizing individual data trends over time, showing the rise and fall of values which helps in identifying trends at a glance.

Stacked Area Charts

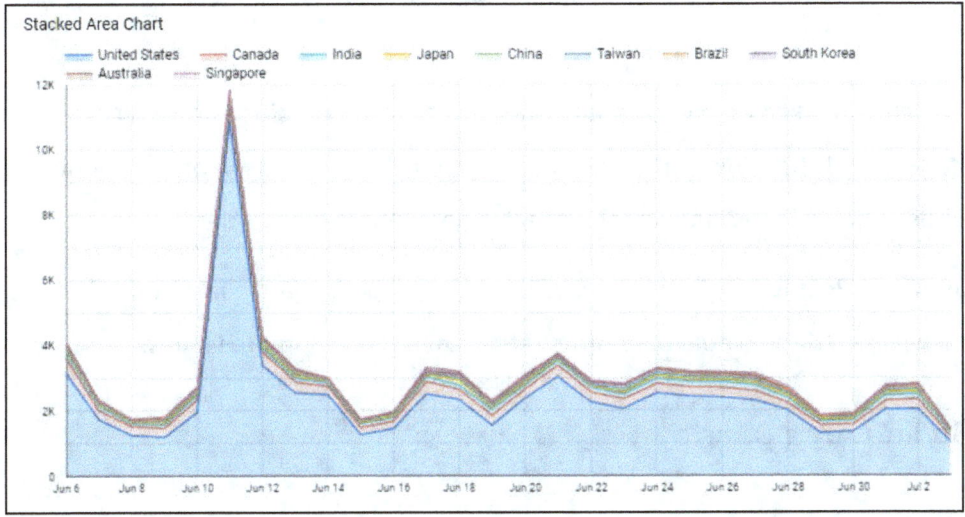

Figure 81. Stacked area chart

These layer the quantities of various data series on top of each other, accumulating the values, which allows the total and the individual contributions to be observed simultaneously.

Use Case: Useful when you need to show how multiple contributions stack up to a total over time, highlighting both the overall trend and the size of each contributor.

100% Stacked Area Charts

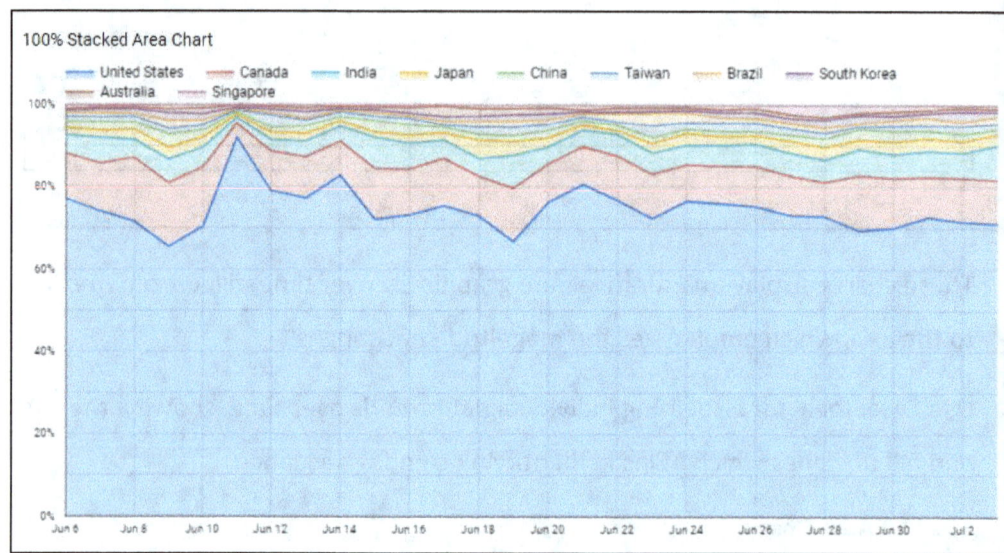

Figure 82. 100% stacked area chart

Similar to stacked area charts but scaled so that the combined area always represents 100%. This normalization allows for the comparison of distribution across categories by showing the relative percentage of each series.

Use Case: Best used when the focus is on the proportionate contributions of each series to the whole over time, rather than their absolute values.

Styling Area Charts

Styling for area charts in Looker Studio can significantly enhance the readability and effectiveness of your data presentation. Here are key styling options available:

Color Settings
Customize the color of each series in the chart to make distinctions clear or match company branding. This includes setting opacity to ensure that overlapping areas are visible.

Line Settings
Adjust the thickness and style of the lines that outline the areas, which can help in distinguishing between different series more clearly.

Point Settings
Optionally add points to the line to highlight exact data values at regular intervals. This can be particularly useful in dense datasets where specific values need to be marked.

Labels and Fonts
Customize labels for clarity and impact. This includes selecting appropriate font sizes, colors, and styles, ensuring that the data speaks with the intended emphasis.

Background and Borders
Set the chart background and border styles to align with the overall design of the dashboard. Options include adjusting border radius, color, and thickness to fit the visual context of the report.

These styling elements not only improve the aesthetics but also enhance the functionality of the charts by making them easier to interpret and more aligned with the intended narrative of the data.

Scatter Visualizations

Scatter plots are invaluable tools in data visualization for examining the relationships between two variables. They provide a straightforward visual assessment of how one variable is affected by another, helping to identify trends, patterns, or outliers within the data. Here's a brief overview of how to utilize scatter plots effectively in Looker Studio.

- **Correlation Analysis**: Scatter plots are perfect for examining the correlation between variables. Whether positive, negative, or null, these relationships can inform business strategies and operational adjustments.

- **Outlier Detection**: Easily spot outliers in your scatter data. These can indicate data entry errors, unusual events, or other anomalies that require further investigation.

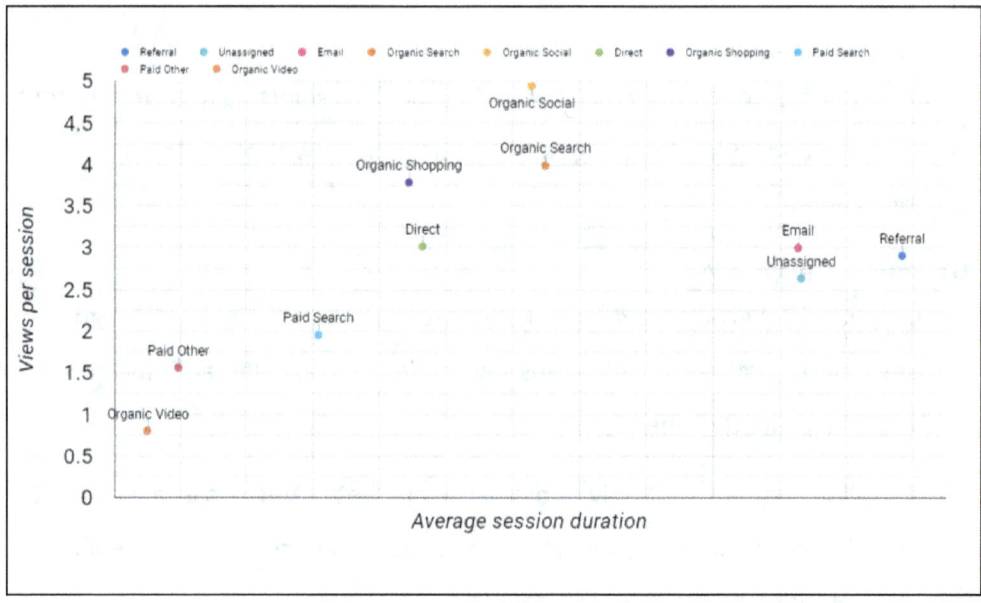

Figure 83. Scatter plot chart

Scatter plots use Cartesian coordinates to display values for two variables for a set of data. The data is displayed as a collection of points, each representing the value of one variable determining the position on the horizontal axis and the value of the other variable determining the position on the vertical axis.

Key Configurations

Bubble Chart

It is possible to set any of the two metrics or use a third metric to control the size of the bubbles in the chart. In the example below in addition to the X-Axis metric "Average session duration" and Y-Axis metric "Views per session", we would like to validate if there is any additional correlation with the "Events per session" metric for the session primary channel group.

Figure 84. Scatter chart with bubbles

Data Axis

Configure your scatter plot by selecting metrics for the X and Y axes. This defines what data is plotted.

Dimensionality

You can add up to three dimensions to your scatter plot, allowing you to group data points by categories like region or product type, which adds depth to your analysis.

Trend Lines: Include trend lines in your scatter plots to identify the general direction of the data points, helping you understand the relationship between the variables.

Styling Scatter Plots

Point Customization

Adjust the size and color of the points to reflect different data categories or magnitudes, making the plot easier to read and more informative.

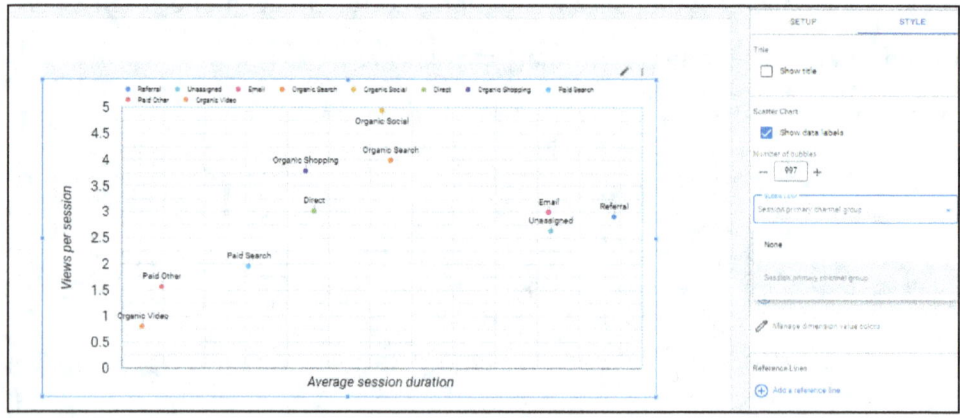

Figure 85. Scatter chart with colored dots

Trendline Axes and Grid

Figure 86. Scatter chart with a trendline

134

In case the color of the buboes is set to none, it is possible to set a trendline to show on the chart. It can either be linear, exponential, or polynomial.

Fine-tune the display of axes, labels, and grid lines to enhance readability. You can set the range, label formatting, and appearance of your plot's axes and grid.

Labels and Legends

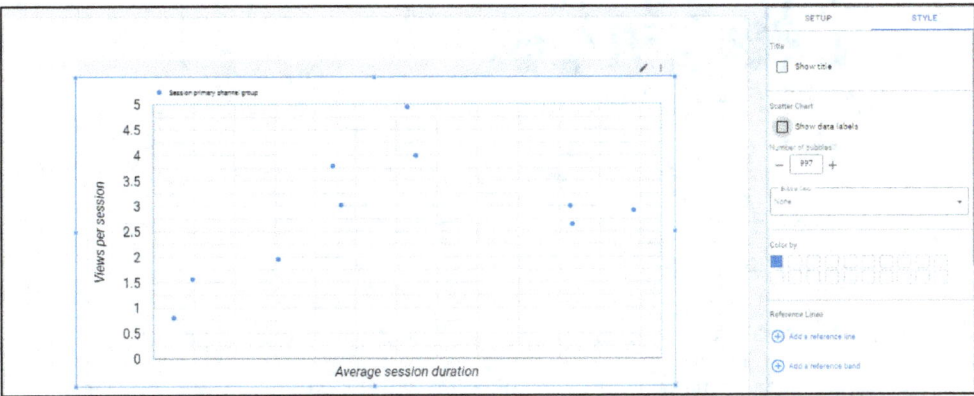

Figure 87. Scatter chart without any labels or colors

Other than the bubble color if applicable, for your chart to be meaningful, you can show the data labels on the chart. Enhance your scatter plot with clear labels and legends that explain the data and variables being displayed, ensuring that the viewer can easily understand the chart's content.

Bullet Charts Visualization

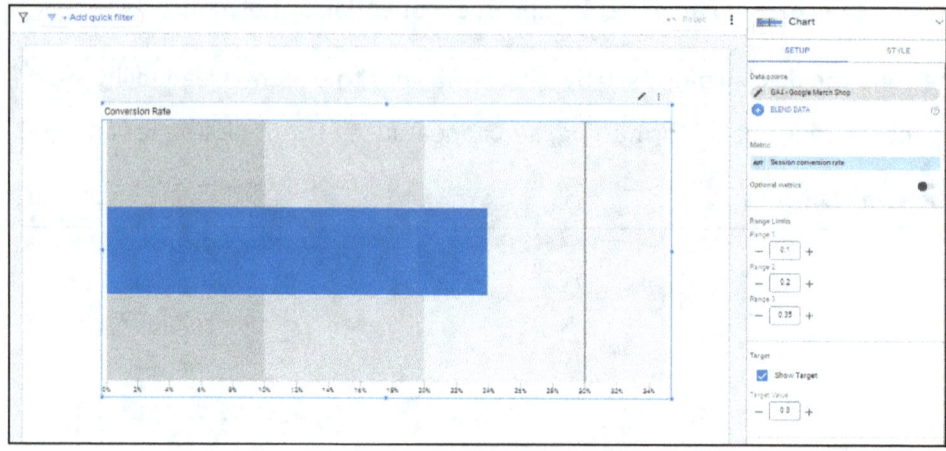

Figure 88. Bullet chart with ranges

Bullet charts are a one of the simplest, yet and efficient ways to display performance data against a set of qualitative ranges (such as poor, average, good) and a quantitative target. They are ideal for dashboards where space is at a premium and where simple, clear presentation of data progress against goals is required.

Bullet charts provide a compact, bar-gauge-like display of KPIs by combining multiple data representations into a single visual form. They are primarily used for:

- **Performance Measurement**: Quickly assess the performance of a metric against predetermined targets.
- **Comparative Analysis**: Compare and contrast performance across different categories or time periods.
- **Efficiency Monitoring**: Monitor progress efficiently without the clutter of traditional bar graphs or complex gauges.

Key Components

- **Metric Bar**: Displays the actual value of the key metric.
- **Target Marker**: A vertical line that shows the goal or target value.
- **Ranged Background**: Divided into colored bands representing different performance thresholds (e.g., red for poor, yellow for average, green for good), which help in quick visual assessment.

Setting Up a Bullet Chart

To create a bullet chart in Looker Studio:

- **Select the Chart Type**: Choose the bullet chart option when adding a new visualization.
- **Metric Configuration**: Define the metric that will be evaluated.
- **Target Setting**: Specify the target value for the metric.
- **Ranges Definition**: Set up to three distinct ranges to visually represent different levels of performance.

Styling Options

- **Color Customization**: Adjust the colors of the metric bar and the range bands to align with the visual language of the dashboard or corporate branding.
- **Target Customization**: Style the target marker to make it stand out or blend in, depending on its importance in the visualization context.
- **Size and Layout Adjustments**: Configure the size of the chart and the spacing to ensure it fits well within the dashboard layout.

Gauge Chart Visualizations

Gauge charts provide a quick, clear way to visualize performance against a predefined target, similar to how bullet chart's function. These charts are particularly useful for displaying key performance indicators (KPIs) in a visually engaging manner.

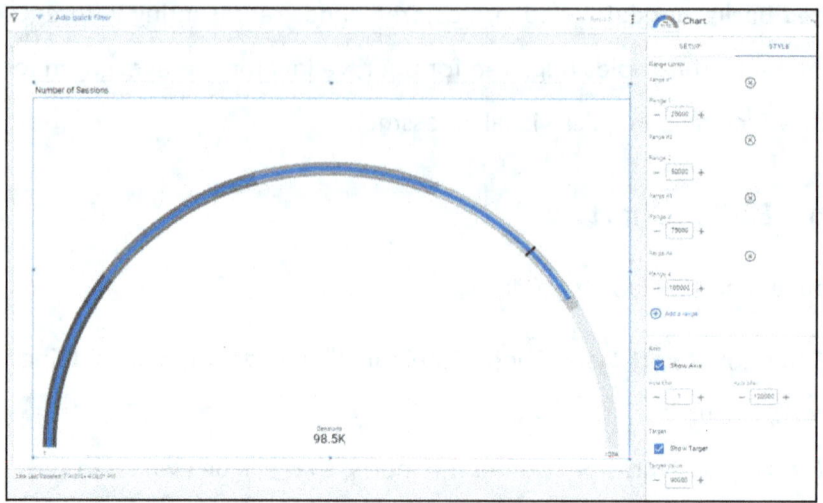

Figure 89. Gauge chart with ranges

Description and Uses

Gauge charts in Looker Studio come in two variations: a simple gauge and a gauge with a range. Both types are used to monitor the health or performance of a metric within a dashboard:

- **Simple Gauge**: Displays a single metric value with a target and optionally compares it to a previous period.
- **Gauge with Range**: Includes color-coded bands (e.g., poor, average, good) which visually represent threshold ranges, adding context to the metric's performance.

These charts are excellent for real-time monitoring of metrics such as sales performance, resource utilization, or progress towards goals, making them indispensable for executive dashboards or operational monitoring.

Configuration

To set up a gauge chart:

- **Metric Configuration**: Choose the metric for display. This metric acts as the primary focus of the gauge.
- **Target and Ranges**: Optionally set a target value and up to five ranges to contextualize the metric's value.

Styling

Styling options for gauge charts allow for customization to fit the aesthetic of any dashboard:

- **Bar Colors**: Customize the color of the central value bar and the threshold ranges.
- **Comparison Metrics**: If comparisons are enabled, configure colors to reflect positive or negative changes.
- **Axis Configuration**: Adjust the minimum and maximum values displayed on the gauge for precise control over the scale.
- **Additional Styling**: Choose fonts, colors, and text sizes for titles and labels to ensure the gauge chart is clear and matches the dashboard's design.

Gauge charts are a straightforward yet powerful tool for at-a-glance performance assessments, similar to bullet charts but often with a more immediate visual impact due to their circular design and color usage.

Treemap Charts

Treemaps are an effective way to visualize hierarchical data in a compact, space-efficient format. They represent data in nested rectangles (or nodes), where each branch of the hierarchy is given its own rectangle, size, and color based on quantitative variables.

Description and Uses

Treemaps are particularly useful for displaying large amounts of hierarchical data in a way that highlights proportions and patterns at multiple levels of the hierarchy. This makes them excellent for:

- **Comparative Analysis**: Quickly comparing different segments and their sub-segments in terms of size and other metrics.
- **Pattern Recognition**: Identifying patterns across complex datasets, such as sales distributions across product categories.
- **Resource Allocation**: Viewing resource distribution across different departments or projects to assess balance or imbalance.

Variations in Treemaps

Treemaps can display data in various ways, including:

Standard Treemaps
Show simple hierarchical structures without emphasizing specific branches.

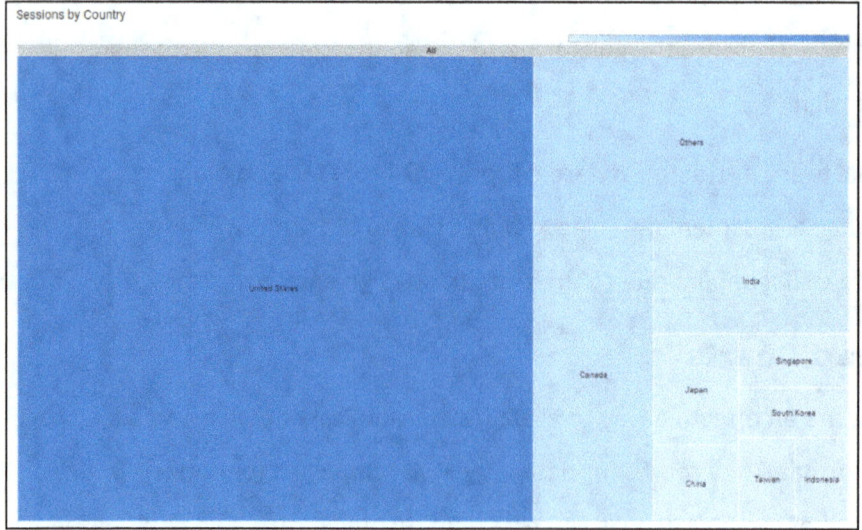

Figure 90. Treemap chart

Nested Treemaps

Each branch is clearly separated and nested within its parent, helping to visualize deeper hierarchy levels.

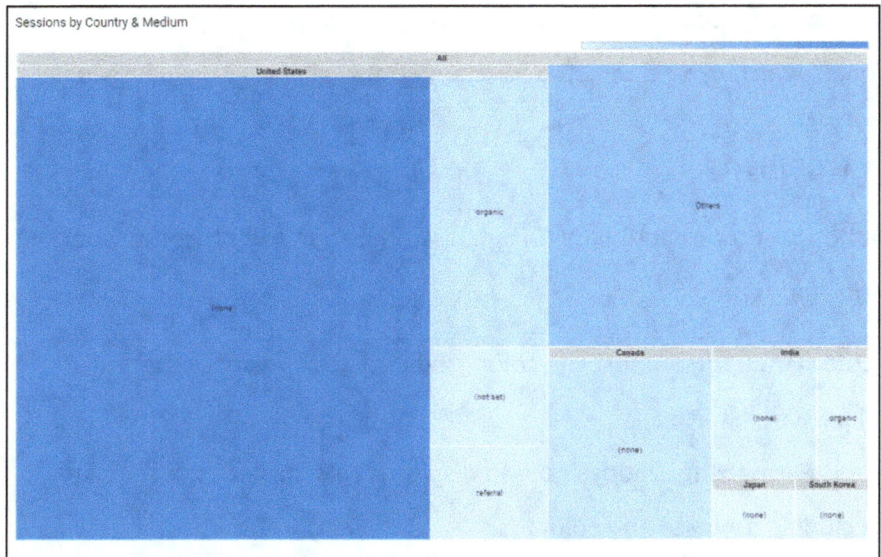

Figure 91. Nested treemap

Key Components

- **Branches/Nodes**: Represent different categories. The size of each node can represent a metric such as sales volume or profit margin.
- **Color Coding**: Can be used to represent different metrics or to highlight categories, making it easier to distinguish between them visually.
- **Drill Down Capability**: Allows users to click on a node to see more detailed data for that particular segment of the hierarchy.

Configuring Treemaps

Setting up a treemap involves:

- Selecting a Data Source: Choose where the data is coming from.

- Defining Dimensions and Metrics: Select which dimensions represent the hierarchical levels and which metric the size of the rectangles should represent.
- Customizing Levels: Decide how many levels of the hierarchy to show at once, which can be adjusted for clarity or detail.

Styling Treemaps

Styling options for treemaps allow further customization to fit them into various dashboards and reports:

- **Color Gradients**: Adjust the color gradients to represent different ranges of data clearly.
- **Text Formatting**: Choose how to display labels for better readability, including font size and color.
- **Borders and Backgrounds**: Define borders and backgrounds to make individual nodes stand out or blend into the overall dashboard design.

Sankey Charts Visualization

Sankey charts are powerful visual tools in Looker Studio that show the flow and distribution of data across different stages or categories. They are particularly useful for visualizing the movement or transfer of quantities between different nodes, making them ideal for depicting processes, migrations, or flow pathways.

Sankey charts are used to represent many-to-many relationships between two or more domains or to illustrate multiple pathways through stages. For instance, they can effectively showcase:

- **Migration patterns**: Visualizing movement between locations, such as migration between cities or traffic flow between website pages.
- **Resource allocation**: Displaying how resources flow through different departments or a process flow as part of the user experience.

- **Customer journey**: Mapping out the various paths customers take between phases within a service or product lifecycle.

These charts are characterized by their nodes and links where the width of each link is proportional to the flow rate or volume of the moved quantity, providing an immediate visual impression of transport or transformation magnitudes.

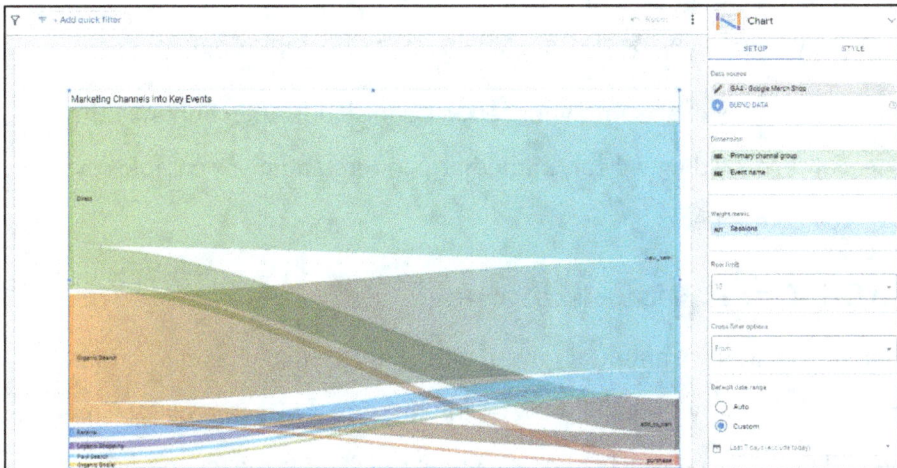

Figure 92. Sankey chart

Configuration

To set up a Sankey chart in Looker Studio:

- **Define Dimensions**: You need at least two dimensions—source and target—to represent the flow's start and end points.
- **Set the Metric**: The metric, often a count or sum, determines the weight or thickness of the links, representing the magnitude of flow between the nodes.

Styling

Sankey charts in Looker Studio offer several styling options to enhance readability and aesthetics:

- **Colors**: Customize the color of nodes and links to differentiate between different data streams or categories.
- **Interactivity**: Enable interactions like hovering to reveal additional data, or clicking to filter other visualizations based on the selected node or link.
- **Layout Adjustments**: Optimize the placement of nodes and the curvature of links for clearer visualization of complex networks.

Incorporating Sankey charts into your reports can significantly enhance the analytical value, providing a clear, immediate understanding of complex systems and their key components.

Waterfall Chart Visualizations

Waterfall charts are instrumental for visualizing sequential changes in data. They are used primarily to depict how an initial value is affected by intermediate positive and negative values, leading to a final result. This makes them particularly useful for financial analysis, such as visualizing profit and loss or cash flow within a given period.

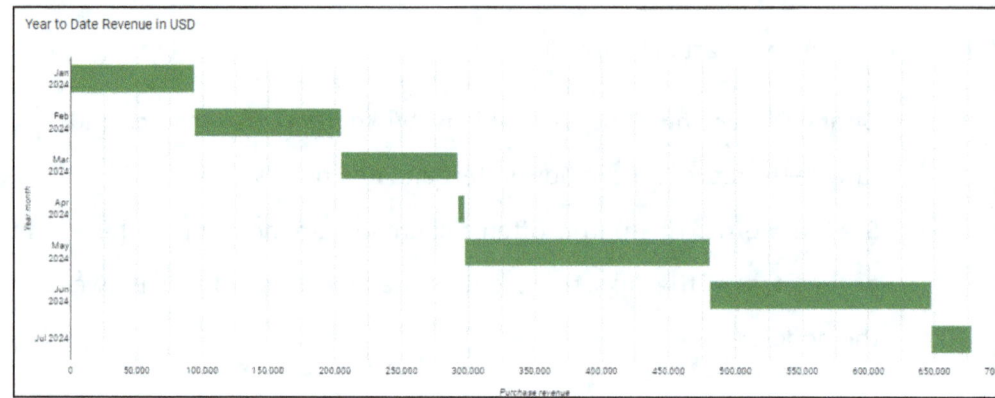

Figure 93. Waterfall chart

Waterfall charts break down the cumulative effect of sequentially introduced positive or negative values. This visualization helps in understanding the gradual transition of a value, providing clear insights into which components had the most impact. For example:

Waterfall charts break down the cumulative effect of sequentially introduced positive or negative values. This visualization helps in understanding the gradual transition of a value, providing clear insights into which components had the most impact. For example:

- **Financial Performance**: Showing how starting revenue is influenced by various costs and operational activities to result in net profit.
- **Timeline Analysis**: Tracking how visits or any other metrics are adjusted through the year.
- **Inventory or Project Tracking**: Demonstrating how project stages or inventory levels build up or decrease over time due to various factors.

Configuration

Setting up a waterfall chart involves Metric and Dimension Setup: Selecting the metric to display and ordering dimensions to depict the flow of data correctly.

Styling

The style tab for waterfall charts offers several options to tailor the visual appearance to better fit the dashboard's theme:

Color Customization: Assign colors to different types of increases or decreases to enhance readability and visual impact.

Data Labels: Optionally show data labels on each segment to provide exact value information.

Connectors: Style the connectors between bars for better visual flow and clarity.

Start and End Caps: Highlight the start and end points with distinct colors or labels to emphasize the beginning and final values.

Waterfall charts are exceptionally effective in scenarios where understanding the step-by-step development of a value is crucial, making them a staple in financial reporting and performance analysis dashboards.

Timeline Chart Visualizations

Timeline charts are an essential tool for visualizing the duration and relationships between various events over a specified period. These charts are particularly useful in displaying sequences and their overlap, making them indispensable in project management, historical data presentation, and process tracking.

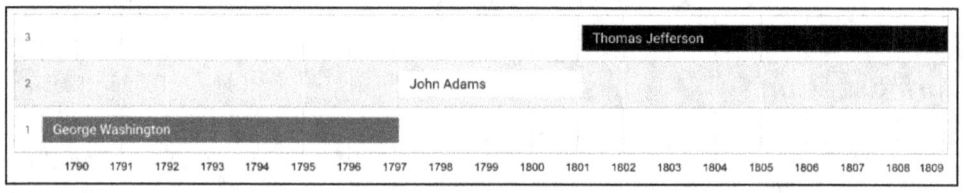

Figure 94. Timeline chart

Configuration Overview

Timeline visualizations are typically unusual to use in Marketing Analytics. To set up a timeline chart in Looker Studio, you need:

- **Row Label**: This is a dimension that acts as a descriptor for each timeline entry, such as an event name or a project stage.
- **Start Time**: A date dimension that marks the beginning of the period.
- **End Time**: Another date dimension that defines the end of the period. Alternatively, you can use a Duration field specified in units (like hours or days), but not both.

Practical Use Cases

- **Project Management**: Track phases of a project from initiation to completion, visualizing overlaps and dependencies.
- **Event Planning**: For events with multiple concurrent sessions or milestones, timelines help stakeholders see the schedule at a glance.
- **Historical or Sequential Data Presentation**: Excellent for showing historical events in education, allowing students to visualize periods and significant events on a timeline.

Styling Options

The styling tab allows you to customize the appearance of your timeline chart:

- **Color Coding**: Distinguish between different types of events or stages by color.
- **Bar Labels**: Optionally add labels to the bars for clarity, which is useful when the Row Label alone isn't descriptive enough.

Building Interactive Dashboards

> Learn how to enhance your dashboards with interactivity using Looker Studio. Understand the importance of filters, chart controls, and dynamic elements to create engaging, user-driven data visualizations.

Interactive dashboards are crucial in transforming static data visualizations into engaging, dynamic tools that enable users to delve deeper into their data. By integrating interactivity, dashboards can offer tailored insights and foster a more exploratory approach to data analysis. This section explores essential techniques and best practices for creating interactive dashboards that not only display data but also allow users to interact with it. Through strategic use of filters, chart level controls, and dynamic elements, these dashboards empower users to manipulate data visualizations in real-time, making them more effective and personalized.

Filters in Interactive Dashboards

Filters are essential tools in interactive dashboards, enabling users to refine and adjust the data displayed according to specific criteria. By implementing various types of filters, you can significantly enhance the interactivity and user engagement of your dashboard.

Styling filters is possible, the same way other charts and components can be styled from the "Style" tab on the right-side panel. It is possible to change modify the text, headers, background, borders, and any other available elements in terms of colors, fonts, transparency, border shapes, and radiuses.

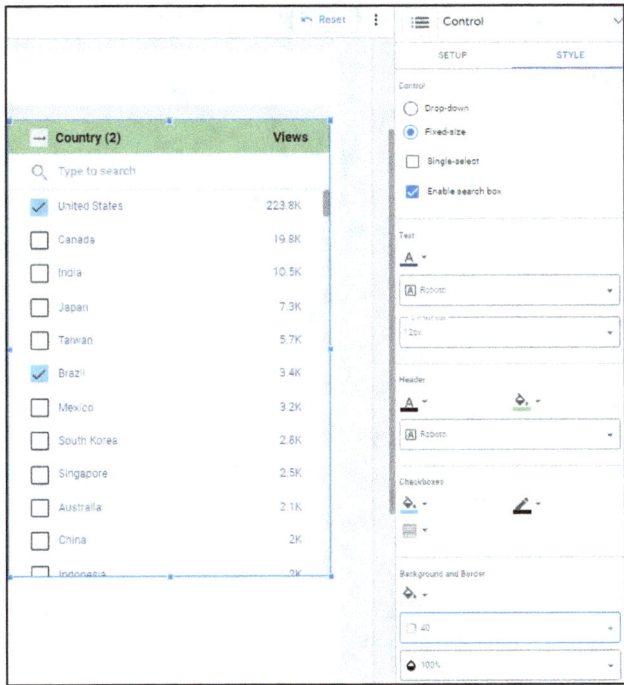

Figure 95. Filter with styling options

Here's an overview of common filter types and their applications:

Date Range Controls

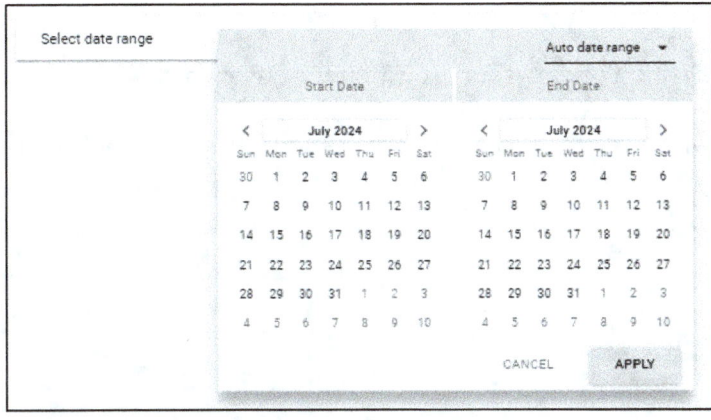

Figure 96. Date range controller

Purpose: Allows users to select a specific date range for the data displayed.

Use Case: Ideal for dashboards tracking time-sensitive data, such as sales performance or website traffic over a period.

Data Controls

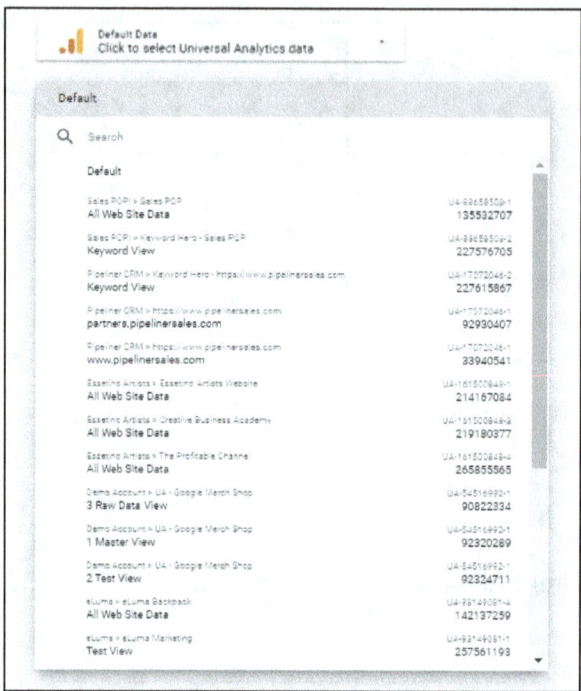

Figure 97. Data controller

Purpose: Enable the selection of data sources within the dashboard.

Use Case: Useful for switching between different data sources such as different Google Analytics accounts.

Dimension Controls

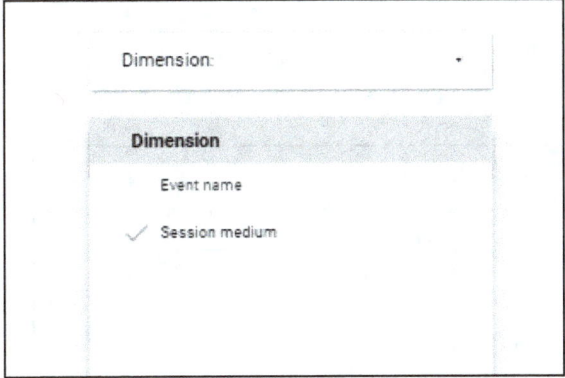

Figure 98. Dimension controller (filter)

Purpose: Lets users filter data based on specific dimensions like geographic location, product categories, or customer segments.

Use Case: Enhances user experience by allowing detailed analysis on different facets of the data.

Buttons

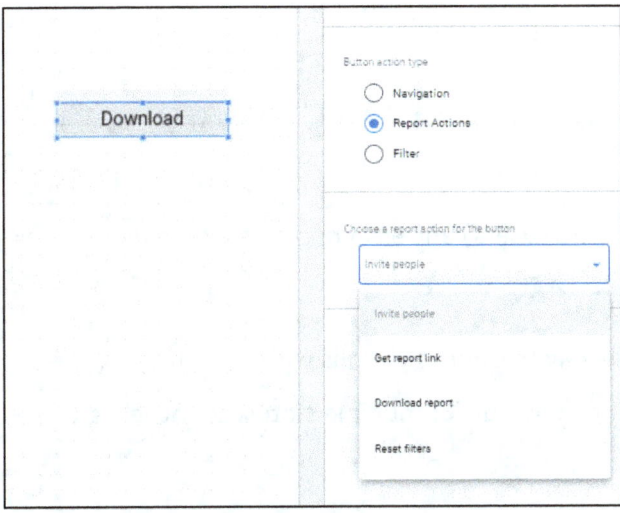

Figure 99. Custom button

Purpose: Triggers specific actions or filter applications in the dashboard.

Use Case: Can be used to navigate to other pages or external links, download data, reset filters to default, or filter the data.

Dropdown List

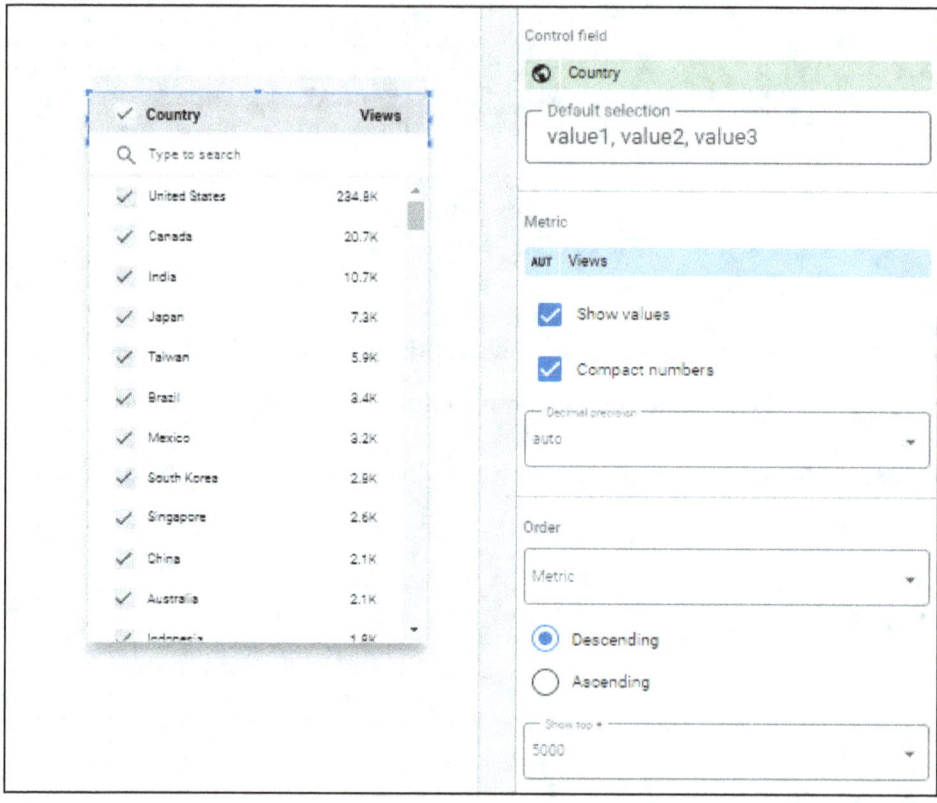

Figure 100. Dropdown list

Purpose: Provides a list from which users can select one or multiple items of a dimension as filters.

Use Case: Compact and simple way to offer selections without cluttering the dashboard, perfect for selecting individual or multiple states, countries, etc.

Fixed Size List

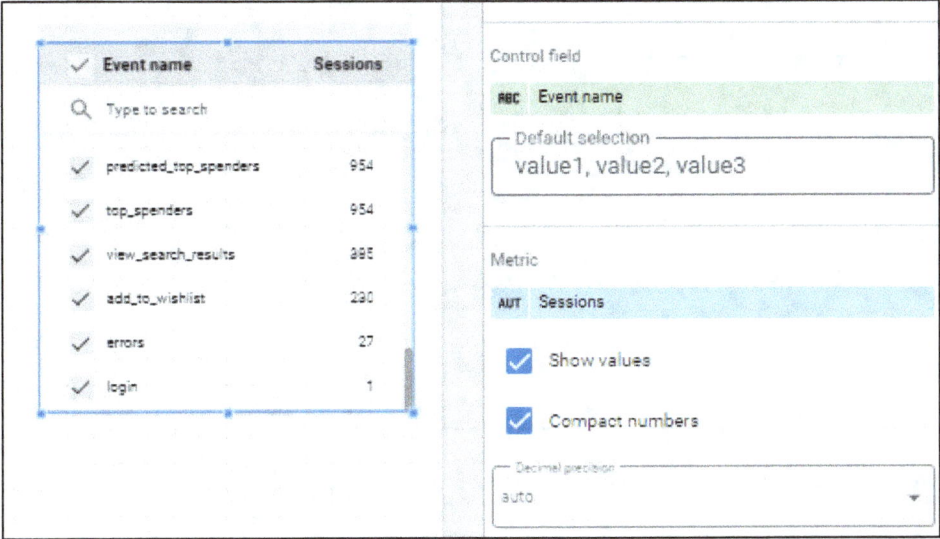

Figure 101. Fixed size list

Purpose: Displays a fixed number of available options, with users able to select one or more.

Use Case: Best for environments where the dataset categories are limited and predefined, like statuses or flags. It is similar to the drop-down list in function, and it just displays the option in a fixed size.

Input Boxes

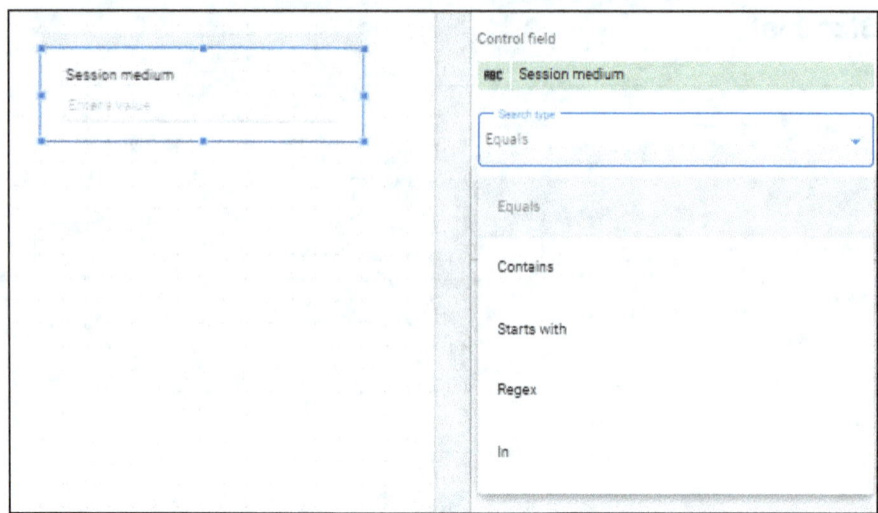

Figure 102. Input box

Purpose: Allows users to enter specific values to search or filter data.

Use Case: Effective in searching for specific items, such as product names, IDs, or other unique identifiers.

Advanced Filters

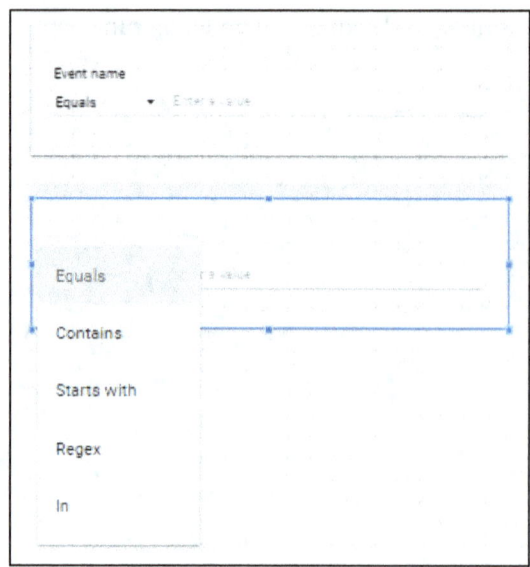

Figure 103. Advanced filter options

Purpose: Offers complex filtering options that might combine multiple filter types into one, allowing for detailed and layered data queries.

Use Case: Suitable for advanced users who need to perform complex queries, such as combining several data points or conditions.

Integrating Hyperlinks within Dashboards

Hyperlinks within dashboards provide users with direct access to additional resources or related data (pages within the dashboard), enhancing the interactive experience. These can be configured within text or image elements, allowing for straightforward.

Text Hyperlinks

These allow users to click on textual elements which are configured to direct them to other pages within the dashboard or external websites. This feature is useful for linking to more detailed reports or external resources.

Image Hyperlinks

Images can be made clickable, similar to text, and configured to link to internal pages or external URLs. This can be particularly engaging when using logos or icons, enhancing both the aesthetic and functionality of the dashboard by providing intuitive navigation aids.

Building in Figma & Translating Designs to Looker Studio Dashboards

> This chapter will guide you through the steps in using Figma for designing high-fidelity dashboards and effectively translating these designs into Looker Studio.

As elaborated earlier, using a collaborative design tool is crucial for the successful design of dashboards. Such tools excel in facilitating teamwork, allowing multiple designers to work on the same project in real time. This collaboration is especially beneficial in the early stages of a dashboard design, where brainstorming and iterative feedback are vital.

Figma for instance offers a versatile platform that enables designers to create high-fidelity prototypes that closely mimic the final product. This ensures that stakeholders can visualize and interact with the design as it will appear in the deployed environment, leading to more accurate feedback and fewer revisions.

The benefits of effectively translating these designs into Looker Studio are manifold. Firstly, it ensures that the visual intent of the design is maintained, preserving the user experience as envisioned during the design phase. Secondly, it streamlines the development process as designers can provide developers with clear, implementable specifications. Lastly, maintaining design fidelity helps in achieving a consistent brand image across all tools and platforms used by a company, reinforcing brand recognition and trust among users.

Step-by-Step to Building High Fidelity Dashboards in Figma

Setting up Your Figma Environment for Dashboard Design

Start by organizing your Figma environment to optimize the design process. Create a new project specifically for dashboards and set up a design system with reusable components and style guides. This includes defining color schemes, typography, and grid layouts that align with your brand standards.

Utilize frames to set device resolutions that will be used, ensuring your dashboard is screen size choice is the most suitable according to the final users' preferences. This initial setup helps maintain consistency throughout the design process and speeds up the creation of new pages of the dashboard.

Key Components to layout in a Dashboard

- **Charts**: Integrate various chart types such as bar, line, pie, and area charts. Design these components with scalability in mind, so they remain readable and functional at different data scales and screen sizes.
- **Controls**: Include interactive elements like sliders, toggle switches, and dropdown menus to allow users to customize data displays according to their preferences. Ensure these controls are accessible and easy to manipulate.
- **Navigation**: Design a clear and intuitive navigation system that guides the user through different sections of the dashboard. Use sidebar menus, tabs, and breadcrumb trails to enhance user experience and facilitate easy access to different dashboard panels.

Utilizing Figma's Features to Create Detailed and Interactive Dashboard Elements

- Rely on vector tools to create custom shapes and icons that enhance the visual appeal of your dashboard. Use the constraints and layout grids to ensure elements are well-aligned and adapt well to different screen resolutions.

- Implement prototyping features to simulate interactions within your dashboard. This includes linking different frames to demonstrate the flow from one section to another, showing hover states for clickable elements such as drop-down filters, and integrating transitions such as chart level drill downs.
- Collaborate in real-time, allowing team members to provide instant feedback on designs. Use commenting feature to gather and incorporate feedback directly on the design files.

Preparing Your Designs for Export

Begin by preparing your designs to ensure they are ready for integration into Looker Studio. This involves 'slicing' components you wish to export, organizing them efficiently, and applying consistent naming conventions that will simplify the import process. This step is crucial for maintaining organization and ease of access to the various design elements within Looker Studio.

Importing Assets into Looker Studio and Setting Up the Dashboard

Once your assets are properly prepared, the next step is to import them into Looker Studio. This involves uploading the graphical elements (such as icons, backgrounds, and layout components) and arranging them according to the planned dashboard layout. During this phase, ensure that each element is positioned and scaled correctly to match the original design.

Handling Font Rendering Issues

Differences in font rendering between design tools and Looker Studio can affect the appearance of text. To minimize issues, use web-safe fonts that are consistently rendered across platforms, or embed custom fonts directly into

Looker Studio if the platform supports it. Additionally, verify text properties such as size, weight, and line spacing to ensure they closely match your design specifications.

Handling Element Sizing

Discrepancies in element sizing can occur due to scaling issues or resolution differences. To maintain consistency, define clear dimensions for each component in Figma using pixels, which can be directly translated to Looker Studio. Check alignment, padding, and spacing needed for Looker Studio to ensure that all elements align with the grid and layout as planned in Figma.

Chapter Recap

- **Set Up Figma Environment**: Organize your workspace, create reusable components, and define style guides for consistency.

- **Design Key Components**: Layout charts, controls, and navigation elements for scalability and user-friendly interaction.

- **Utilize Figma Features**: Use vector tools, prototyping features, and real-time collaboration to enhance design detail and interactivity.

- **Prepare Designs for Export**: Slice and organize components with consistent naming conventions for easy import.

- **Import into Looker Studio**: Upload and arrange graphical elements, ensuring correct positioning and scaling.

- **Font Rendering**: Use web-safe fonts or embed custom fonts to ensure consistent text appearance.

- **Element Sizing**: Define clear dimensions in pixels and check alignment, padding, and spacing for consistency across platforms.

Final Words

As we wrap up this guide on building marketing analytics dashboards using Figma and Looker Studio, it's clear that the integration of robust design practices with advanced data visualization techniques is not merely about crafting appealing interfaces but is essential for crafting strategic tools that empower marketers to make data-driven decisions.

Throughout this book, we've delved into several aspects of dashboard creation—from initial design sketches in Figma to their final realization in Looker Studio. We've covered the nuances of interactivity that enhance user engagement, the subtleties of maintaining visual fidelity during design translation, and the critical role of effective communication in dashboard design. By exploring the intersection of aesthetics and functionality, we've seen how effectively designed dashboards can transform raw data into compelling stories that drive strategic business actions.

Using collaborative design tools underscores the importance of collaboration and flexibility in design, enabling teams to iterate quickly and refine dashboards in real-time, ensuring that the end products are not only visually coherent but also aligned with marketing objectives and user needs. The transition of these designs into Looker Studio has revealed the practical challenges and solutions involved in maintaining consistency across platforms, ensuring that every element from fonts to color schemes works harmoniously to support data comprehension and user experience.

This book highlights the strategic implications of well-designed marketing dashboards. In today's data-driven marketing landscape, these dashboards serve as pivotal tools for understanding consumer behavior, tracking marketing ROI, and adjusting strategies in real-time. They enable marketers to harness the power of their data to create targeted, effective campaigns that resonate with audiences and yield measurable outcomes.

As we conclude, remember that the field of data visualization and dashboard design is ever-evolving. The techniques discussed here should serve as an inspirational foundation to explore innovation. Continue to push the boundaries of what can be achieved with creative and analytical thinking combined. The journey from design to data isn't just about creating functional tools—it's about inspiring smarter, more strategic marketing decisions that can propel businesses forward in a competitive landscape.

Let this book be both a resource and an inspiration as you continue to explore the intersection of design, data, and marketing. Embrace new challenges, collaborate across disciplines, and keep innovating. The future of marketing is bright, and continuously evolving. With the right tools at your disposal, and right approach you are well-prepared to light the way forward.

Table of Figures

Figure 1. A digital product prototype example ___ 12

Figure 2. Low-fidelity design ___ 15

Figure 3. High-fidelity design ___ 16

Figure 4. Dashboard main interface designed in Figma ___ 18

Figure 5. Chart single components designed in Figma ___ 19

Figure 6. Impact of color in dashboard design ___ 30

Figure 7. Importance of suitable chart type selection ___ 30

Figure 8. Visual hierarchy impact ___ 31

Figure 9. Appropriate use of icons and titles to describe charts' content ___ 32

Figure 10. Marketing dashboard with appropriate chart types such as a marketing funnel, and other relevant visualizations with proper titles and icons ___ 33

Figure 11. Executive dashboard low-fidelity sketch ___ 44

Figure 12. Marketing dashboard low-fidelity sketch ___ 45

Figure 13. Wireframe example of a software UI basic sketch ___ 51

Figure 14. Visual examples of ineffective layouts ___ 58

Figure 15. Looker Studio dashboard example with a visible header ___ 69

Figure 16. Low-fidelity sketch of a single page dashboard without any navigation menu ___ 70

Figure 17. Low-fidelity sketch of a single page dashboard with a custom left-side navigation menu ___ 71

Figure 18. Looker Studio dashboard header with page navigation arrows ___ 71

Figure 19. Looker Studio dashboard with a native top side navigation menu _ 72

Figure 20. Looker Studio dashboard with a native left side navigation menu _ 73

Figure 21. Time range drop down controller ___ 77

Figure 22. Dimensions drop down filters ___ 77

Figure 23. Top-left corner dashboard logo ___ 78

Figure 24. Basic shapes and lines on a dashboard canvas grid _____ 78

Figure 25. Custom made dark theme _____ 83

Figure 26. Setting a custom theme Step 1 _____ 85

Figure 27. Setting a custom theme Step 2 _____ 85

Figure 28. Setting a custom theme Step 3 _____ 86

Figure 29. Setting a custom theme Step 4 _____ 86

Figure 30. Chart type selection _____ 87

Figure 31. Table chart style adjustment _____ 88

Figure 32. Table chart with dimension drill down arrows shown in the table header _____ 89

Figure 33. Table chart with optional metrics selection shown in the table header _____ 90

Figure 34. Table chart with metric sliders _____ 90

Figure 35. Table header options _____ 90

Figure 36. Styling the grid _____ 91

Figure 37. Setting border and background styles _____ 92

Figure 38. General chart styling _____ 93

Figure 39. Pasting styles on a chart _____ 94

Figure 40. Different table chart variations _____ 95

Figure 41. Table data different visualizations formats _____ 96

Figure 42. Long table fading heatmap data style _____ 97

Figure 43. Vertical vs. horizontal table chart alignment _____ 98

Figure 44. Pivot table with heatmap data styling _____ 98

Figure 45. Scorecard with previous period comparison and a trend line _____ 99

Figure 46. Scorecard variations: full number (basic scorecard) vs. a compact number _____ 100

Figure 47. Decimal precision adjustment for a compact scorecard _____ 101

Figure 48. Previous period comparison as a percentage _____ 102

Figure 49. Previous period comparison as an absolute number _____ 102

Figure 50. Previous period comparison as an absolute compact number ___ 103

Figure 51. Previous period comparison with a hidden label _____ 103

Figure 52. Previous period comparison with a custom label_____ 104

Figure 53. Scorecard with "Date" as a sparkline dimension _____ 105

Figure 54. A scorecard with modified sparkline color _____ 105

Figure 55. A scorecard with a sparkline filled area _____ 106

Figure 56. A scorecard with a smooth sparkline _____ 106

Figure 57. A scorecard with a progress visual indicator _____ 107

Figure 58. Time series chart with a previous period comparison _____ 108

Figure 59. Time series variations examples _____ 109

Figure 60. Time series chart with one of the series showing as a bar _____ 110

Figure 61. Plotted data points on one of the series_____ 111

Figure 62. Showing captions on one of the series _____ 111

Figure 63. One of the series shown as a stepped line _____ 112

Figure 64. Adding a trend line to one of the series _____ 112

Figure 65. Adding an interval area to the chart _____ 113

Figure 66. Adding a reference line to the chart_____ 113

Figure 67. Different variations of bar and column charts _____ 115

Figure 68. Adding data labels to a column chart _____ 117

Figure 69. Adding a reference line indicator to a column chart _____ 119

Figure 70. Pie visualization variations: Full pie vs. donut chart_____ 119

Figure 71. Adjusting the donut ring _____ 122

Figure 72. Map visualization with bubbles _____ 122

Figure 73. Map with bubbles _____ 124

Figure 74. Filled map _____ 124

Figure 75. Heat map_____ 125

Figure 76. Lines map _____ 125

Figure 77. Connection map _____ 126

Figure 78. Combo Map _____ 126

Figure 79. Geo chart (filled map) _____ 127

Figure 80. Area chart _____ 129

Figure 81. Stacked area chart _____ 129

Figure 82. 100% stacked area chart _____ 130

Figure 83. Scatter plot chart _____ 132

Figure 84. Scatter chart with bubbles _____ 133

Figure 85. Scatter chart with colored dots _____ 134

Figure 86. Scatter chart with a trendline _____ 134

Figure 87. Scatter chart without any labels or colors _____ 135

Figure 88. Bullet chart with ranges _____ 136

Figure 89. Gauge chart with ranges _____ 138

Figure 90. Treemap chart _____ 140

Figure 91. Nested treemap _____ 141

Figure 92. Sankey chart _____ 143

Figure 93. Waterfall chart _____ 144

Figure 94. Timeline chart _____ 146

Figure 95. Filter with styling options _____ 149

Figure 96. Date range controller _____ 149

Figure 97. Data controller _____ 150

Figure 98. Dimension controller (filter) _____ 151

Figure 99. Custom button _____ 151

Figure 100. Dropdown list _____ 152

Figure 101. Fixed size list _____ 153

Figure 102. Input box _____ 154

Figure 103. Advanced filter options _____ 154

www.ingramcontent.com/pod-product-compliance
Lightning Source LLC
Chambersburg PA
CBHW071830210526
45479CB00001B/67